# ROMANTIC PARADOX

# ROMANTIC PARADOX

## An Essay On
## The Poetry of Wordsworth

by
### C. C. CLARKE

**GREENWOOD PRESS, PUBLISHERS**
WESTPORT, CONNECTICUT

**Library of Congress Cataloging in Publication Data**

Clarke, Colin Campbell.
 Romantic paradox.

 Reprint of the 1963 ed. published by Barnes &
Noble, New York.
  1.  Wordsworth, William, 1770-1850--Criticism and
interpretation.  2.  Perception in literature.
I.  Title.
PR5888.C5  1979      821'.7      78-10859
ISBN 0-313-20758-5

Reprinted with the permission of Routledge & Kegan
Paul Ltd.

Reprinted in 1979 by Greenwood Press, Inc.
51 Riverside Avenue, Westport, CT 06880

Printed in the United States of America

10  9  8  7  6  5  4  3  2  1

FOR
ANN AND ANTONIA

# ACKNOWLEDGEMENTS

I WISH to thank Frank Kermode, Peter Ure, J. C. Maxwell, Edward Khamara and Herbert Piper, who read various sections of this essay in typescript and from each of whom I have received encouragement and valuable advice.

My thanks are due also to the editor of *English Studies* (Amsterdam), who has given me permission to use material from an article which I contributed to his journal in 1950 (Vol. XXXI). I have drawn upon this material on pages 88 to 92.

> . . . I still
> At all times had a real solid world
> Of images about me . . .
>
> *The Prelude*

ASSUMPTIONS about the mind and its place in nature are concealed in every act of human perception. We take it for granted, merely by perceiving or being aware, that the given world both is and is not extrinsic to our selves, and that through what goes on within our own experience we can know things as they really are, or as they would be if unknown. As Lovejoy observed in *The Revolt Against Dualism*, 'man . . . is by nature an epistemological animal', whose 'irrepressible knowledge-claim', far from being an invention of philosophers, is a manifestation of his own 'primary and most universal faith . . ., his inexpugnable realism'. The human being cherishes the

> 'two-fold belief that he is on the one hand in the midst of realities which are not himself nor mere obsequious shadows of himself, a world which transcends the narrow confines of his own transient being; and, on the other hand, that he can somehow reach beyond those confines and bring these external existences within the compass of his own life, yet without annulment of their transcendence.'

In other words, however rational the systems of the professional philosophers may or may not be, and however free from contradiction, it is implied in the perceptual experience of the ordinary, unreflective observer that the place of mind in the natural world is equivocal, or a paradox.

I shall try to show in the following pages that a more or less latent awareness of this paradox, a feeling for the ambiguity and the strangeness of perception, a largely unconscious perplexity in fact, was the 'cause' of some of Wordsworth's finest poetry; and that this perplexity shaped the meanings he gave to the crucial words 'image' and 'form', which he applied so often to the configuration of the visible world. My subject, in short, is the way the poetry articulates what Wordsworth himself called 'questionings of sense'.

## II

HOBBES appears to have been the first to use the word 'image' to mean 'immediate object of visual perception': in the second chapter of *Human Nature* he denies that 'the Image in Vision' exists out there in the external world. And yet by the very act of raising the question at all he reminds us that the image at any rate *seems* to exist objectively, and that, at the very least, it is associated as closely with outward objects as with mind or sensation. Indeed this is an instance of what Mr. Blackmur refers to in *Language As Gesture* when he speaks of words dragging 'after them into being their own opposites'. 'Image', 'picture' and 'scene', when used of objects present to sight, suggest the meaning '*things*-imaged' (or pictured or seen) as well as 'image *of* things'.

The relevant passage in *Human Nature* runs:

'by *Sight* we have a Conception or Image composed of *Colour* and *Figure*, which is all the notice and knowledge the Object imparteth to us of its nature by the Eye.

Because the *Image* in Vision consisting of *Colour* and *Shape* is the knowledge we have of the qualities of the Object of that sense; it is no hard matter for a man to fall into this Opinion, that the same *Colour* and *Shape* are the *very qualities* themselves. . . . And this Opinion hath been so long received, that the *contrary* must needs appear a great Paradox; and yet the introducing of *Species visible* and *intelligible* (which is necessary for the maintenance of that Opinion) passing to and fro from the *Object*, is *worse* than any Paradox as being a plain *impossibility*. I shall therefore endeavour to make plain these Points:

That the Subject wherein Colour and Image are inherent, is *not* the *Object* or thing seen.

That there is nothing *without us* (really) which we call an Image or Colour.

That the said Image or Colour is but an *Apparition* unto us of the *Motion*, agitation or alteration which the *Object* worketh in the *Brain*, or spirits, or some internal substance of the head.'

It will be observed that Hobbes admits that there are good *prima facie* reasons for 'confusing' the image and the qualities of the object itself.

This admission that the true, philosophical way of thinking about the image does not correspond with our deepest prejudices reappears in a different guise in Addison's Essays on *The Pleasures Of The Imagination*, for though he follows Hobbes and Locke in drawing a distinction between objects (or their qualities) and images (or ideas) he does not sustain the distinction with full philosophical rigour. An unadmitted willingness to recognize that images inhere in things-themselves betrays him into occasional inconsistencies of expression; while his distinction between two *kinds* of image, the one 'actually . . . in view' and the other stored in the mind or fabricated from materials provided by memory ('We cannot indeed have a single image in the fancy that did not make its first entrance through the sight') only confirms the reader's common-sense assumption that an image in the first sense exists 'in the mind' in a radically different way from an image in the second sense. It is significant that Addison uses the word 'object' both of material things and immediate objects of perception, as Locke (but without confusion) had before him. ('External Objects, furnish the Mind with the Ideas of sensible Qualities', *Essay* 11.1.5; 'Whatsoever the Mind perceives in it self, or is the immediate Object of Perception, Thought or Understanding, that I call Idea', *Essay* 11.8.8.) Here are some examples of Addison's equivocal or near-equivocal use of 'object'—the first four from Essay 1 and the others from Essay 2:

'Our sight is the most perfect and most delightful of all our senses. It fills the mind with the largest variety of ideas, converses with its objects at the greatest distance, and continues the longest in action without being tired or satiated with its proper enjoyments'.

'. . . by "the pleasures of the imagination" or "fancy" (which I shall use promiscuously) I here mean such as arise from visible objects, either when we have them actually in our view, or when we call up their ideas into our minds by paintings, statues, descriptions, or any the like occasion.'

'. . . my design being first of all to discourse of those primary pleasures of the imagination, which entirely proceed from such objects as are before our eyes . . .'

'It is but opening the eye, and the scene enters. The colours paint themselves on the fancy, with very little attention of

4

thought or application of mind in the beholder. We are struck, we know not how, with the symmetry of any thing we see, and immediately assent to the beauty of an object, without enquiring into the particular causes and occasions of it.'

'I shall first consider those pleasures of the imagination which arise from the actual view and survey of outward objects'.

'Our imagination loves to be filled with an object, or to grasp at any thing that is too big for its capacity'.

The language here is at once naïve and sophisticated. For instance, when it is remarked that 'we assent to the beauty of an object,' what we are said to recognize as beautiful, given the premises of the argument, must be an image, an immediate object of perception—an interpretation that tends to be borne out by the statement, 'The colours paint themselves on the fancy. . . .' And yet it is clear that what Addison means here first of all by object is 'material thing': 'We are struck, we know not how, with the symmetry of any thing we see. . . .' And in effect he suggests throughout the essays that landscapes, scenes, or prospects—the equivalents of images—are virtually as objective (i.e. extrinsic to the subject perceiving them) as things themselves. The language in the following passage, for example—casual, non-specialist, as imprecise as everyday speech—contrives to imply that the 'prospect' is no more private and inward than the fields themselves:

'A man of a polite imagination is let into a great many pleasures that the vulgar are not capable of receiving. He can converse with a picture, and find an agreeable companion in a statue. He meets with a secret refreshment in a description, and often feels a greater satsifaction in the prospect of fields and meadows than another does in the possession.'

Addison's distinction between images and the qualities of objects serves in fact a rhetorical rather than a philosophical purpose: it is a way of focusing attention on his essential subject-matter—namely, aesthetics. For image tends to imply picture; and picture, beauty. But any significance that the distinction between images and things might have beyond this is not his concern. And indeed he need not have occupied himself with the distinction at all. For the subject of 'taste' or 'the picturesque' can be discussed without supplying a philosophical framework; and it does not follow from the fact that objects of perception compose themselves into pictures that the pictures are subjective. (For further comments on the use of the word 'image' in eighteenth century aesthetics see an article by Ray Frazer in *ELH*, June 1960.)

The tendency to confuse images (or prospect or picture) on the one hand and natural objects on the other, even when ostensibly distinguishing between them, is of minor significance within the context of Addison's essays themselves. But it begins to assume more importance when we observe its bearing on the poetry first of Akenside (I consider his work in the following section) and then of Wordsworth, whose landscapes often exist simultaneously as prospects within the mind, as outward scenes, and as configurations of solid objects.

> . . . and, when a lengthened pause
> Of Silence came and baffled his best skill,
> Then sometimes, in that silence while he hung
> Listening, a gentle shock of mild surprise
> Has carried far into his heart the voice
> Of mountain torrents; or the visible scene
> Would enter unawares into his mind,

With all its solemn imagery, its rocks,
Its woods, and that uncertain heaven, received
Into the bosom of the steady lake.

These lines are quoted in the O.E.D. to illustrate a meaning of
'imagery' that emerged about the time Hobbes published
*Human Nature*: viz. 'scenery, or nature's image-work'. (The
earliest instance recorded in the Dictionary is dated 1647.) But
in fact in the context of Wordsworth's poetry the meaning of
the word is much less circumscribed than the Dictionary suggests. For 'It is one of those words which, looked at, gets ahead
of all its uses and makes something unexpected of its context,
as words in poetry should.' (I quote again from *Language As
Gesture*, where it is the work of Yeats that is in question.) The
primary meaning of 'imagery' and 'image' in Wordsworth's
poetry is generally familiar enough—viz. outward or inward
'picture'—but the words often tug against these simple meanings in the direction of something more complicated and interesting. In the lines under review the language effectively
cancels sharp disjunctions between spatial and mental dimensions ('far into his heart'), or mind and the things it perceives,
or imagery and things imaged. The uncompromising ap-
position '. . . its solemn imagery, its rocks, Its woods' implies
a simple equivalence of imagery and outward objects and
suggests that if it is not quite the rocks and woods themselves
that enter the mind neither is it a mere picture or representation of them.

Indeed, it will become more and more apparent as we proceed that Wordsworth found the status of images deeply
puzzling, though his perplexity is not, for the most part, ex-
pressed discursively, but through indirections of meaning and
ambiguities. At its best his landscape poetry is richly equivocal:
a proof that he found the language of the sense itself equivocal.

7

And this proof is not less convincing because the double meanings generally have the air of being fortuitous, and often seem
to evolve under the casual pressure of the syntax. It is worth
recalling the famous remark in the Fenwick note to *Ode.
Intimations Of Immortality*, a note that has a relevance extending
far beyond the *Ode* itself:

> '. . . I was often unable to think of external things as having
> external existence, and I communed with all that I saw as
> something not apart from, but inherent in, my own im-
> material nature. Many times while going to school have I
> grasped at a wall or tree to recall myself from this abyss of
> idealism to the reality.'

The 'visible scene', in the lines quoted above, exists outwardly
along with the rocks and woods of which it is composed; and
yet it enters the mind as though it were of the same stuff as the
mind. In other words it resembles the scenes that perplexed
the child. For all their concreteness Wordsworth's landscapes
are often hauntingly insubstantial. It is as though he were
poised between a realist reading of his world and a purely
subjective one.

His poetry then has genuine affiliations with philosophy;
but affiliations only. Indeed a pointer to the sense in which his
work may be called philosophical is provided by the Fenwick
note already quoted, for his use of the word 'idealism' in that
note is a case of epistemology being submerged in the present-
ment of a concrete perceptual situation. The concept of 'idealism' was commonly associated, then as now, with a sophisticated technique of reasoning or a corpus of ideas, or (finally)
with the pursuit of ideals in literature, art or moral life; and
there was no precedent for Wordsworth's applying it to particular, felt acts of perception. His usage of course recalls
Berkeley and other phenomenalists (though Berkeley used the

words 'idea' and 'ideal' and never the derivative 'ideal-ism'). Still there is novelty in the way Wordsworth resorts to the abstract noun to establish a meaning that is anything but abstract, subordinating theory to sensation, the notional to the experiential. For he gives us the feel of a solipsistic moment without showing any interest in Solipsism.

It has already been implied that Wordsworth's 'perplexity', inherited from childhood, could only have been augmented by the intellectual climate in which he grew up. The doctrine that sense-images exist in the mind and do not belong out there in nature raises very sharply the question how they can be so specific (i.e. have the solidity, particularity and fullness of detail that we habitually ascribe to material things). Certainly Hume's distinction between degrees of *vivacity* in impressions would not have settled the problem. For Hume, as for Locke and Berkeley, there was nothing paradoxical about the fact that the world-as-perceived should be substantial (that is, extended and solid) and also subjective. But if, like Wordsworth, we retain a layman's faith in the independent existence of everything—or virtually everything—given to sense, and yet remain covertly convinced that what the senses know is an attribute of *consciousness* (I use this notoriously imprecise term advisedly, for the old Cartesian confusion of consciousness and the *content* of consciousness reflects a radical uncertainty in the mind of the ordinary observer) then we may well find perceptual experience contradictory. We are reminded of the criticism which Berkeley directed against the epistemology of Locke—an epistemology which from Berkeley's point of view amounted to an illogical compromise.

'By matter therefore we are to understand an inert, senseless substance, in which extension, figure and motion, *do actually subsist*. But it is evident from what we have already shown, that extension, figure, and motion, are *only ideas existing in the mind*, and that an idea can be like nothing but another idea, and that consequently neither they nor their archetypes can exist in unperceiving substance. Hence it is plain, that the very notion of what is called *matter*, or *corporeal substance*, involves a contradiction in it.'

(*Treatise* 1, ix)

But this contradiction, which to Berkeley was merely a product of false reasoning, was to Wordsworth part of the nature of things, a dilemma felt on the pulses. His conviction that the natural world is solid, and substantially 'other' than the mind that contemplates it, had to come to terms with his conviction that what we perceive is inevitably mind-dependent. A dramatic tension in his poetry was frequently the result.

The fact that this dilemma was so important in the poetic life of Wordsworth assumes a wider significance when we find that an attempt to resolve precisely the same dilemma is the main impulse behind the philosophic writings of Coleridge. Since Coleridge was the representative English philosopher of his time, so radical a similarity between his case and Wordsworth's would seem to tell us something especially significant about the Romantic sensibility: i.e. the kind of new 'life' the Romantics had to offer.

Because Coleridge refused to deny either that it is things themselves that we know, and not mere copies of things, *or* that the existence of what we know is implicated with acts of consciousness, his metaphysics may be described, in the paradoxical phrase of the friend whom he quotes in Chapter XIII of the *Biographia*, as 'ideal Realism'. Holding firmly to his two convictions, first 'that there exist things' outside the self and second that 'I am', he tackles the problem how

'. . . something essentially different from ourselves, nay even in opposition to ourselves . . . could possibly become a part of our immediate consciousness; in other words, how that which *ex hypothesi* is and continues to be extrinsic and alien to our being should become a modification of our being'.

His solution of the problem is transcendentalist; but his transcendentalism is very much bound to the earth.

'. . . the apparent contradiction, that the former position, namely, the existence of things without us, which from its nature cannot be immediately certain should be received as blindly and as independently of all grounds as the existence of our own being, the transcendentalist philosopher can solve only by the supposition, that the former is unconsciously involved in the latter; that it is not only coherent but identical, and one and the same thing with our own immediate self-consciousness. To demonstrate this identity is the office and object of his philosophy.'

He goes on to distinguish his theory from what seemed to him the spurious realism and spurious idealism of his day.

'If it be said that this is idealism, let it be remembered that it is only so far idealism, as it is at the same time, and on that very account, the truest and most binding realism. For wherein does the realism of mankind properly consist? In the assertion that there exists a something without them, what, or how, or where they know not, which occasions the objects of their perception? Oh no! This is neither connatural or universal. It is what a few have taught and learnt in the schools, and which the many repeat without asking themselves concerning their own meaning. The realism common to all mankind is far older and lies infinitely deeper than this hypothetical explanation of the origin of our perception, an explanation skimmed from the mere surface of mechanical philosophy. It is the table itself, which the man of common sense believes himself to see, not the phantom of a table, which he does not see. If to destroy the reality of all that we actually behold, be idealism, what can be more egregiously so than the system of modern metaphysics, which banishes us to a land of shadows, surrounds us with apparitions, and distinguishes truth from illusion only by the majority of those who dream the same dream?'

(*Biographia*, Chapter XII)

There is real point in associating these philosophical speculations of Coleridge with the poetry of Wordsworth. In *Tintern Abbey*, the first book of *The Excursion*, and very often in *The Prelude*, we find a poetic 'equivalent' of Coleridge's 'ideal Realism' in the sense that there, in the dialectic of his verse, Wordsworth resolves the apparent contradiction that the natural world is extrinsic to the self and yet a modification of it. Resolves it, however—if I may be allowed to labour the point a little—in the manner of a poet. The questionings of sense are seldom fully explicit—much less literal or reasoned—questionings. Though the grown man was almost as perplexed by his sensations as the child, it was mostly at a level of the mind where consciousness is barely conceptualized. And for this reason Wordsworth's preoccupation with the relation of inner to outer may be called not so much a characteristic or bias of his mind as, in Jamesian language, its 'very atmosphere'. Occasionally, it is true, the perplexity found expression on the surface of the poetry rather than just beneath it:

> Oh 'tis a joy divine on summer days
> When not a breeze is stirring, not a cloud,
> To sit within some solitary wood,
> Far in some lonely wood, and hear no sound
> Which the heart does not make, or else so fit(s)

To its own temper that in external things
No longer seem internal difference
All melts away, and things that are without
Live in our minds as in their native home.

(*Vide* Volume V of the Oxford edition, Appendix B.) But in
the following pages I shall be concerned for the most part with
poetry in which Wordsworth is not *explicitly* puzzled and not
recording perceptions that are unlike normal perceptions. The
'mystical' moments in *Tintern Abbey* for instance are validated
by, and find their primary analogue in, quite ordinary sensory
experiences in which the visible scene and the observer's mind
at once confront each other (preserving their distinctions) and
interpenetrate deeply.

### III

BECAUSE he was preoccupied with what the mind does
with the materials offered by the senses, Wordsworth shows
a predilection not only for the word 'image' but for the word
'form', and, to a less extent, the word 'shape'; for the images
of nature which the mind receives and stores are the 'colours
and the forms' (or shapes) of visible landscapes. It will be an
effective way of coming at what is novel in his landscape-
poetry to give an account of his usage of these three words;
and this in turn will involve an account of the way the words
were used in the poetry preceding his own. To provide this
however we need go no further than Akenside's *The Pleasures
Of The Imagination*—though consideration will also be given

to passages in *Night Thoughts* and *The Minstrel*. Akenside uses the word 'form' much more frequently and suggestively than any other eighteenth-century poet, and it is clear that it was he first and foremost who supplied Wordsworth with the *literary* stimulus (as distinct from the experiential) for his formulation, or re-creation, of the paradox of sense-perception. It is interesting to watch Akenside groping at this paradox. Only once, or perhaps twice—in the revised version—does he make memorable poetry out of it. In this as in other matters Wordsworth took over where Akenside left off.

But I begin (ignoring chronological order) with a passage from *Night Thoughts* (6.413 ff.):

> Where, thy *true* treasure? Gold says 'Not in *me:*'
> And, 'Not in me,' the di'mond. Gold is poor;
> *India's* insolvent; Seek it in *thyself,*
> Seek in thy naked self, and find it there;
> In *being* so descended, form'd, endow'd;
> Sky-born, sky-guided, sky-returning race!
> Erect, immortal, rational, divine!
> In *senses*, which inherit earth, and Heav'ns;
> Enjoy the various riches *Nature* yields;
> Far nobler; *give* the riches they enjoy;
> Give taste to fruits; and harmony to groves;
> Their radiant beams to gold, and gold's bright fire:
> Take in, at once, the landscape of the world,
> At a small inlet, which a grain might close,
> And half create the wondrous world they see.
> Our *senses*, as our *reason*, are divine.
> But for the magic organ's pow'rful charm,
> Earth were a rude, uncolour'd chaos, still.

> *Objects* are but th'occasion; our's th'*exploit*;
> Our's is the cloth, the pencil, and the paint,
> Which Nature's admirable picture draws;
> And beautifies creation's ample dome.
> Like *Milton's Eve*, when gazing on the lake,
> Man makes the matchless image, man admires.
> Say then, Shall man, his thoughts all sent abroad,
> (Superior wonders in himself forgot)
> His admiration waste on objects round?
> When Heav'n makes him the soul of all he sees?
> Absurd! not rare! so great, so mean, is man.

The attention shifts from landscape to objects, to picture, to image and back to objects. In other words the poetry is incipiently paradoxical; and for this reason—and not merely because Young used an expression that is partly recalled in *Tintern Abbey*—it points forward to Wordsworth.

The contradictions inherent in sense-perception are sometimes exploited by Young in a manner that is arresting but lacking in poetic tact.

> How great,
> How glorious, then, appears the Mind of man,
> When in it all the stars, and planets, roll!
> And what it seems, it is: Great objects make
> Great minds, enlarging as their views enlarge;
> Those still more Godlike, as These more divine.
> (*Consolation*, 1059)

He does violence here to the reader's conviction that natural objects are extrinsic to the mind that perceives them. This sort of extravagance was something the mature Wordsworth was never guilty of. But we know that in the early part of his career he was fond of Young's work (see Potts: *Wordsworth's*

15

*Prelude*) and it is likely that he owed to him something of the habit of referring to mental events in spatial terms. ('There littleness was not . . . What wonder if his being thus became Sublime and comprehensive!'; 'far-stretching views of immortality'; and so on.) In accounting for the meaning that the word 'image' came to have for Wordsworth, at least some weight must be attached to the influence of *Night Thoughts*.

I turn now to the more important document for my purposes: *The Pleasures Of The Imagination*. (Unless otherwise stated all references are to the first edition.)

Akenside uses the word 'image' to mean 'effigy' (1.109); 'mental picture' (11.191, 111.14); and 'embodiment of an eternal archetype' (1.308, 1.322), and hence an 'emblem'. But we get a good deal closer to Wordsworth with this usage:

> For when the different images of things
> By chance combin'd, have struck the attentive soul
> With deeper impulse, or connected long,
> Have drawn the frequent eye; howe'er distinct
> The external scenes, yet oft the ideas gain
> From that conjunction an eternal tie,
> And sympathy unbroken.
>
> (111.312)

Although the images draw the frequent *eye* and so, we presume, are to be conceived of as existing outwardly, they also have power to penetrate—can strike with 'deeper' impulse. Taken in conjunction with 'external', the word 'deeper' implies, if only faintly, that the dimensions of the soul are at once mental and spatial. Indeed a writer who sets out to record the behaviour of images will inevitably make use of terms normally applied to external objects, with the result that, unwittingly, he will do at least some justice to the general human assumption that what the observer sees in nature is both detached from him and part of his mental experience.

My next example is clearly less relevant to a study of Wordsworth, but still has a bearing on it. (Akenside is describing the process by which works of fancy or art come into being):

> Colours mingle, features join,
> And lines converge: the fainter parts retire;
> The fairer eminent in light advance;
> And every image on its neighbour smiles.
>
> (III.405)

These images are of a conventional enough kind (they are unequivocally inward), and yet they are minor harbingers of the images we find in the poetry of Wordsworth, for they stir with life and are potentially mobile.

However it is not so much the word 'image' as the word 'form' that Akenside finds most congenial to his purposes:

> Alas! in such a mind,
> If no bright forms of excellence attend
> The image of his country . . .
>
> (III.36)

'Platonic idea': this is the primary meaning that the word held for him. (Compare Beattie's *The Minstrel*: 'Those forms of bright perfection' II, xxxix.) He distinguishes between two kinds of form. There are the archetypes of beauty, truth and goodness; and there are the forms that are apparent in the phenomenal world of matter (I.526: 'The forms which brute, unconscious matter wears . . .'). These phenomenal forms can also be grouped into forms in a different sense, viz. species in

17

the hierarchy of nature. There are the 'blooming forms' for instance (1.457): that is, the species of form that bloom.

However his manner of using the word 'form' is not always as stale as this summary—or the following instance—might suggest:

> Is aught so fair
> In all the dewy landscapes of the spring
> In the bright eye of Hesper or the morn,
> In nature's fairest forms, is aught so fair
> As virtuous friendship?
>
> (1.500)

Akenside distinguishes clearly enough here between moral beauty and the beauty of landscape; and yet natural objects as well as virtues have their prototypes in the eternal realm of Being, and the moral awe with which he contemplates this realm carries over sometimes to the phenomenal world which copies or partakes of it—and this makes for interesting complications, and is of obvious relevance to the study of Wordsworth.

> Then the great spirit, whom his works adore,
> Within his own deep essence view'd the forms,
> The forms eternal of created things:
> The radiant sun; the moon's nocturnal lamp;
> The mountains and the streams; the ample stores
> Of earth, of heaven, of nature. From the first,
> On that full scene his love divine he fix'd,
> His admiration; till, in time compleat,
> What he admir'd and lov'd his vital power
> Unfolded into being. Hence the breath
> Of life informing each organic frame:
> Hence the green earth, and wild-resounding waves:
> Hence light and shade, alternate; warmth and cold;

And bright autumnal skies, and vernal showers,
And all the fair variety of things.

(1.106.1772)

The distinction between eternal forms and phenomena has ceased to matter here: objects that exist within the deep essence of the spirit also exist, three-dimensionally, in the world given to sight. This merging of phenomenal and ideal forms takes on further significance when we find elsewhere that this same word 'forms' is used, indifferently, for the visible aspects of external objects and for the impressions left by those objects on a *human* mind:

For to the brutes

    Perception and the transient boons of sense
    Hath fate imparted: but to man alone
    Of sublunary beings was it given
    Each fleeting impulse on the sensual powers
    At leisure to review; with equal eye
    To scan the passion of the stricken nerve
    Or the vague object striking: to conduct
    From sense, the portal turbulent and loud,
    Into the mind's wide palace one by one
    The frequent, pressing, fluctuating forms,
    And question and compare them. Thus he learns
    Their birth and fortunes; how allied they haunt
    The avenues of sense; what laws direct
    Their union; and what various discords rise,
    Or fix'd or casual; which when his clear thought
    Retains and when his faithful words express,
    That living image of the external scene,
    As in a polish'd mirror held to view,
    Is truth; where'er it varies from the shape
    And hue of its exemplar, in that part

19

Dim error lurks. Moreover, from without
When oft the same variety of forms
In the same order have approach'd his mind,
He deigns no more their steps with curious heed
To trace . . .

(11.48.1772)

Because Akenside insists here on the *distance* between the initial impulse and the living image (*avenues* of sense, *approached* the mind) he inevitably presses the word 'forms' into double service (as Wordsworth was to do in the analogous passage in *Tintern Abbey*, 11 23–49). These forms are at once components of nature and impressions on the mind; so their existence is as equivocal as that of the forms within the essence of the great spirit.

Here is a final example:

Else wherefore burns
In mortal bosoms this unquenched hope,
That breathes from day to day sublimer things,
And mocks possession? wherefore darts the mind,
With such resistless ardour to embrace
Majestic forms; impatient to be free,
Spurning the gross controul of wilful might;
Proud of the strong contention of her toils;
Proud to be daring? Who but rather turns
To heaven's broad fire his unconstrained view,
Than to the glimmering of a waxen flame?

(1.166)

These majestic forms are not mountains, but archetypes of moral beauty. Yet their close association with a grand natural object ('heaven's broad fire') is characteristic of a poem in which the eternal Forms and the forms of natural objects are at once blended and dissociated—the blending being largely a matter of implication and the dissociation a matter of assertion. As a result of this double process, and despite the explicit argument of the poem, the majestic or eternal forms, here and elsewhere, become recognizable progenitors of the ostensibly different forms that meant so much to Wordsworth—the forms of mountains, waterfalls, lakes, and so on.

Akenside also uses 'form' to mean a construction of Fancy or art that may or may not correspond with fact (1.139; 111.78) and a phantom or apparition (1.341). But this latter meaning (it was an important one for Wordsworth) is rare in *The Pleasures Of The Imagination*. It is to be found, most obviously, in the Gothic tale and in Milton. (For the influence of Milton see Potts: *Wordsworth's Prelude*, pp. 89–91.) But here is an instance from the work of an eighteenth-century poet:

> Along yon glittering sky what glory streams!
> What majesty attends Night's lovely queen!
> Fair laugh our valleys in the vernal beams;
> And mountains rise, and oceans roll between,
> And all conspire to beautify the scene.
> But, in the mental world, what chaos drear!
> What forms of mournful, loathsome, furious mien!
> O when shall that eternal morn appear,
> These dreadful forms to chase, this chaos dark to clear!
> (*The Minstrel*: 11, xx)

In juxtaposing the beauties of nature and spectral forms in the mind Beattie foreshadows Wordsworth:

> No familiar shapes
> Remained, no pleasant images of trees,
> Of sea or sky, no colours of green fields;
> But huge and mighty forms, that do not live
> Like living men, moved slowly through the mind
> By day, and were a trouble to my dreams.

21

But Wordsworth's usage is a complicated one and I deal with it in detail later.

'Shape'—the last word of the trilogy—is used by Akenside as a synonym for nearly all the separate meanings of 'image' and 'form'. One example will suffice:

> Anon ten thousand shapes,
> Like spectres trooping to the wizard's call,
> Flit swift before him . . .
>
> (III.385)

Here the shapes are both phantoms and memory-images.

These examples—and particularly the lines about 'The frequent, pressing, fluctuating forms . . .' from the version of 1772—should show how thoroughly Akenside had prepared the stage for Wordsworth, though he rarely exploited the paradox of sense-perception with anything approaching Wordsworth's subtlety and power.

## IV

IN his apprentice and journeyman work, composed in the years prior to 1797, Wordsworth used the words 'image', 'form' and 'shape' for the most part in a conventional way. I choose a few examples at random:

Adieu, ye forms of Fear that float
Wild on the shipwreck of the thought,
While fancy in a Demon's form
Rides through the clouds and swells the storm.
                    (*The Vale Of Esthwaite*)

Like Una shining on her gloomy way,
The half seen form of Twilight roams astray
                    (*An Evening Walk*)

In solemn shapes before th'admiring eye
Dilated hang the misty pines on high
                    (*Descriptive Sketches*)

For images of other worlds are there,
Awful the light, and holy is the air
                    (*Descriptive Sketches*)

                    I now perceived
That we are praised, only as men in us
Do recognize the image of themselves.
                    (*The Borderers*)

If Thou be one whose heart the holy forms
Of young imagination have kept pure
                    (*Lines*, left upon a Seat
                    in a Yew-tree)

(These 'holy forms Of young imagination' are essentially
Akenside's 'bright forms of excellence'.)

However these examples tell less than the whole story. For
in the MS additions to *An Evening Walk* which Wordsworth
inserted in 1794 into his own copy (the poem was published
in 1793) we find two passages of reflective verse that point
forward very clearly to the poetry of his maturity; and in
these passages he is beginning to add to the word 'forms' a new

dimension of meaning. These *addenda* were not in fact included in the later editions for which they must have been intended; no doubt because the poetry strains beyond the limits—the conventions of the decorous and picturesque—within which *An Evening Walk* is so obviously contained. We have no manuscript evidence that Wordsworth wrote again in this vein until after the completion of *The Borderers*:

> A heart that vibrates evermore, awake
> To feeling for all forms that Life can take,
> That wider still its sympathy extends
> And sees not any line where being ends;
> Sees sense, through Nature's rudest forms betrayed,
> Tremble obscure in fountain rock and shade,
> And while a secret power those forms endears
> Their social accents never vainly hears.

And:

> Yes, thou art blest, my friend, with mind awake
> To Nature's impulse like this living lake,
> Whose mirror makes the landscape's charms its own
> With touches soft as those to Memory known;
> While exquisite of sense the mighty mass
> All vibrates to the lightest gales that pass.
> And are there souls whose languid powers unite
> No interest to each rural sound or sight,
> To the lone chapel on the ocean coast,
> The nameless brook below in ocean lost,
> The bridge that spans the brook's small bed half-dry,
> And the proud sails in glory sweeping by?
> How different with those favoured souls who, taught
> By active Fancy or by patient Thought,
> See common forms prolong the endless chain

Of joy and grief, of pleasure and of pain;
But chiefly those to whom the harmonious doors
Of Science have unbarred celestial stores,
To whom a burning energy has given
That other eye which darts thro' earth and heaven,
Roams through all space and . . . unconfined,
Explores the illimitable tracts of mind,
And piercing the profound of time can see
Whatever man has been and man can be,
From him the local tenant of the shade
To man by all the elements obeyed.
With them the sense no trivial object knows,
Oft at its meanest touch their spirit glows,
And proud beyond all limits to aspire
Mounts through the fields of thought on wings of fire.

Though the influence of Young, and to a less extent Akenside, is certainly apparent here, there are fleeting moments of a kind of poetry that was beyond the reach of either. Admittedly Wordsworth applies spatial metaphors to the mind in a way that recalls the excesses of *Night Thoughts* ('Mounts through the fields of thought on wings of fire'); but unlike Young he makes a genuinely poetic attempt to bridge the gap between mind and nature. (Young was prone to annihilate the gap by the simple device of denying its existence.) The heart *vibrates*; fountain, rock and shade *tremble* with sense. The verbs, at least partly, convince as naturalistic description, and also go some distance towards persuading us that there is a mysterious affinity between the outward tremblings and the inward vibrations: what is 'sympathy' in the heart is 'secret power' in the rocks etc. Wordsworth is endeavouring to create a shifting linguistic context in which the words 'sense' and 'forms' can be applied, interchangeably and accurately, to mind *and* nature.

The same can be said of the second passage. The lake is a living lake, and so of course is the lake of the mind. Both have depth, and take impressions; both react sensitively at the meanest touch. Because an attempt is made here to create a world in which the dimensions are, indifferently, spatial and mental, the word 'prolong' takes on a more-than-metaphoric force:

> See common forms prolong the endless chain
> Of joy and grief, of pleasure and of pain.

'Prolong' both takes meaning from the word 'forms' and gives it. Because we have been partly persuaded that the forms of nature exist inwardly as well as outwardly, it makes literal sense to speak of the forms *prolonging* human feeling.


In the years 1797–8 Wordsworth discovered his main theme: the place of mind in nature. And at the same time we find him using the words 'image', 'form' and 'shape' with a greatly increased range of suggestion. The relevant pieces for study here are the tale of the discharged soldier, which was later incorporated in *The Prelude*; the tale of *The Pedlar*, as contained in the first extant MS of *The Ruined Cottage*; and some fragments of blank verse to be found in the Alfoxden Note Book.

Here is the account of his meeting with the soldier:

>                 On I went
> Tranquil, receiving in my own despite
> Amusement, as I slowly pass'd along,
> From such near objects as from time to time,
> Perforce, intruded on the listless sense
> Quiescent, and dispos'd to sympathy,
> With an exhausted mind, worn out by toil,

And all unworthy of the deeper joy
Which waits on distant prospect, cliff, or sea,
The dark blue vault, and universe of stars.
Thus did I steal along that silent road,
My body from the stillness drinking in
A restoration like the calm of sleep,
But sweeter far. Above, before, behind,
Around me, all was peace and solitude,
I look'd not round, nor did the solitude
Speak to my eye; but it was heard and felt.
O happy state! what beauteous pictures now
Rose in harmonious imagery—they rose
As from some distant region of my soul
And came along like dreams; yet such as left
Obscurely mingled with their passing forms
A consciousness of animal delight
A self-possession felt in every pause
And every gentle movement of my frame.
    While thus I wander'd, step by step led on,
It chanc'd a sudden turning of the road
Presented to my view an uncouth shape
So near, that, slipping back into the shade
Of a thick hawthorn, I could mark him well,
Myself unseen.

The passing forms in the mind behave so like the near objects
that *intrude* on the listless sense as though they were within the
mind as well as outside it that rigid distinctions between outer
and inner become irrelevant. (The observer steals *along* the
silent road, and the pictures come *along* like dreams; both the
prospect and the region of the soul are *distant*; the outward
solitude is heard and *felt*, the self-possession is *felt* in every
pause; etc.) The uncouth shape that confronts the young man

unawares is located, firmly enough, in the world of the senses; and yet there is a hint that it belongs also to that world of 'intervenient imagery' (to borrow an apt expression from the third book of *The Prelude*) that lies mid-way between the substantial waking world and the world of sleep; or rather embraces them both. In other words the context tends to assimilate the 'shape' to the passing forms in the mind, although the surface narrative makes it clear that it is a three-dimensional shape known to sight.

> He was of stature tall,
> A foot above man's common measure tall,
> Stiff in his form, and upright, lank and lean;
> A man more meagre, as it seem'd to me,
> Was never seen abroad by night or day.
> His arms were long, and bare his hands; his mouth
> Shew'd ghastly in the moonlight: from behind
> A milestone propp'd him, and his figure seem'd
> Half-sitting, and half-standing. I could mark
> That he was clad in military garb,
> Though faded, yet entire. He was alone,
> Had no attendant, neither Dog, nor Staff,
> Nor knapsack; in his very dress appear'd
> A desolation, a simplicity
> That seem'd akin to solitude. Long time
> Did I peruse him with a mingled sense
> Of fear and sorrow. From his lips, meanwhile,
> There issued murmuring sounds, as if of pain
> Or of uneasy thought; yet still his form
> Kept the same steadiness; and at his feet
> His shadow lay, and mov'd not.

The repetition of 'form' and its association with 'lean', 'meagre' and 'shadow' just keeps alive the possibility that the form of the soldier somehow belongs with the passing forms or harmonious imagery in the mind. Although the word 'image' is not in fact applied to the uncouth shape in this original version, it might well have been. In the later version we get:

> How gracious, how benign, is Solitude;
> How potent a mere image of her sway;
> Most potent when impressed upon the mind
> With an appropriate human centre.

The paragraph from which these lines are taken irritates the reader not only because, in de Selincourt's words, 'it was unnecessary, and (because) the rather elaborate style in which it is written contrasts awkwardly with the bare, telling simplicity of the narration that follows' (*Notes*, p. 525), but because it precedes that narration, so that the significance of 'image', the crucial word in this context, seems to be imposed upon the narrative instead of emerging from it unobtrusively. The uncouth shape of the original is an image in the primary sense that it is an object of perception and yet seems to rise out of the perceiver's own consciousness; and beyond this, it is an image or emblem of the potent sway of Solitude. The 'image' of the later version however, which is also—potentially—an image in a double sense (both 'sensation "impressed upon the mind"' and 'type'), is merely abstract, an emblem that is virtually devoid of content and emblematic of nothing.

The next passage I shall consider is to be found early in *The Ruined Cottage*:

> So the foundations of his mind were laid
> In such communion, not from terror free.

While yet a child, and long before his time
He had perceived the presence and the power
Of greatness, and deep feelings had impressed
Great objects on his mind, with portraiture
And colour so distinct (that on his mind)
They lay like substances, and almost seemed
To haunt the bodily sense. He had received
A precious gift, for as he grew in years
With these impressions would he still compare
All his ideal stores, his shapes and forms,
And being still unsatisfied with aught
Of dimmer character, he thence attained
An *active* power to fasten images
Upon his brain, and on their pictured lines
Intensely brooded, even till they acquired
The liveliness of dreams. Nor did he fail,
While yet a child, with a child's eagerness,
Incessantly to turn his ear and eye
On all things which the rolling seasons brought
To feed such appetite. Nor this alone
Appeased his yearning; in the after day
Of boyhood, many an hour in caves forlorn
And in the hollow depth of naked crags
He sate, and even in their fixed lineaments,
Or from the power of a peculiar eye,
Or by creative feeling overborne,
Or by predominance of thought oppressed,
Even in their fixed and steady lineaments
He traced an ebbing and a flowing mind,
Expression ever varying.

In order to convince himself of the solidity and externality of
the visible world, the child Wordsworth 'grasped at a wall or

tree' (just as Dr. Johnson, with the intention of refuting Berkeley, vigorously kicked a stone). And Bonamy Price had this tale to tell of the poet in old age (it is quoted by de Selincourt in his notes to *Ode. Intimations Of Immortality*):

'The venerable old man raised his aged form erect; he was walking in the middle, and passed across me to a five-barred gate in the wall which bounded the road on the side of the lake. He clenched the top bar firmly with his right hand, pushed strongly against it, and then uttered these ever-memorable words: "There was a time in my life when I had to push against something that resisted, to be sure that there was anything outside me. I was sure of my own mind; everything else fell away, and vanished into thought." '

Though a phenomenalist may assure us that the tactile and kinaesthetic senses provide no better proof of the 'otherness' of objects than the sense of sight, the layman instinctively touches things and tests their resistance in order to convince himself that they have substance. (In his book *Looking At Pictures* Sir Kenneth Clark, discussing Vermeer's 'eye', writes: 'For the first, and almost for the last, time in European painting, it is an eye which felt no need to confirm its sensations by touch. The belief that what we touch is more real than what we see is the basis of drawing. A firm outline denotes a tangible concept.') So we shall not be surprised to find that Words-worth, who bears such wavering testimony to the solidity of the natural world, should assure us in one and the same context that images are 'pictured lines' and that they 'lie upon the mind' like things that have weight.

In the 1814 edition of *The Excursion* the lines immediately following 'and deep feelings had impressed' were altered to read:

31

> and deep feelings had impressed
> So vividly great objects that they lay
> Upon his mind like substances, whose presence
> Perplexed the bodily sense.

In a copy of his own Poetical Works (1836–7) which he used for correction and redrafting of his text Wordsworth altered the lines again so as to read:

> and deep feelings had impressed
> Upon his mind great objects so distinct
> In portraiture (lineament), in colouring so vivid
> That on his mind they lay like substances
> And almost indistinguishably mixed
> With things of bodily sense.

And finally in the 1845 edition this is altered once more and becomes:

> and deep feelings had impressed
> Great objects on his mind, with portraiture
> And colour so distinct, that on his mind
> They lay like substances, and almost seemed
> To haunt the bodily sense.

The weakest of these versions is the one published in 1814. The others make it clear that the great objects are not only substances but pictures; and it is the paradoxical relationship between imagery as picture and imagery as substance that the ensuing paragraph is, above all, concerned with. The word 'vividly' in the 1814 edition is insufficiently precise: it leaves us guessing at what seems to have been the intended meaning— namely, that a colourful and sharply defined *picture* lay upon the mind. In the first and the last two versions however we are left face to face with the full paradox of sense-perception: the images lie heavily, like substances, and yet are to be thought of as a kind of portraiture. (Compare *The Prelude*, Book 11.176 ff. 1805.) So when shortly afterwards we come upon the expression 'fixed lineaments', the impression of stability and solidity that the phrase seems so surely to evoke is insensibly qualified, for 'lineaments' recalls 'pictured lines' and so points inwards, if only dimly, as well as outwards. As a result, when the word is used a second time, we are fully prepared to accept the implication that the 'fixed and steady lineaments' are not merely the line of the crags but are lines depicted on a mind. And beyond that, we are ready to respond to the suggestion that this mind is eternal, and that it finds expression in the line of the crags much as the human mind finds expression in the lineaments of the face.

Further on in the *addendum* to *The Ruined Cottage* (Volume V, p. 402) we find the following:

> Or was it ever meant
> That this majestic imagery, the clouds
> The ocean and the firmament of heaven
> Should lie a barren picture on the mind?

What the syntax demonstrably asserts here is that imagery and clouds (and ocean, and firmament) are identical: images are things and things are images. Moreover the imagery has weight and substance, for it *lies* on the mind. But this is only half the story. For the imagery is a mental picture (though a hypothetically barren one) and must therefore be insubstantial. And this picture in turn is also both tenuous and solid, for it lies on the mind just as certainly as the imagery does.

This brings me to one of the most remarkable uses of the word 'image' in the whole of Wordsworth:

> Yet still towards the cottage did I turn
> Fondly, and trace with nearer interest

33

That secret spirit of humanity
Which, 'mid the calm oblivious tendencies
Of Nature, 'mid her plants, her weeds and flowers,
And silent overgrowings, still survived.
The old man, seeing this, resumed, and said
My Friend, enough to sorrow have you given,
The purposes of Wisdom ask no more,
Be wise and cheerful, and no longer read
The forms of things with an unworthy eye.
She sleeps in the calm earth and peace is here.
I well remember that those very plumes,
Those weeds and the high spear-grass on that wall,
By mist and silent rain-drops silvered o'er,
As once I passed, did to my mind convey
So still an image of tranquillity,
So calm and still, and looked so beautiful,
Amid the uneasy thoughts which filled my mind,
That what we feel of sorrow and despair
From ruin and from change, and all the grief
The passing shews of being leave behind
Appeared an idle dream that could not live
Where meditation was. I turned away
And walked along my road in happiness.

The lines make even more impact in *The Excursion* than they
do here in the original version, because the long reflective
argument from the *addendum*—much of which was worked
into *The Excursion* Book IV—is deleted. The decision to
abridge this discourse was a wise one; for the Wanderer's
prolonged reflections had had the effect of partially severing
the moral from the narrative. In the published version we
cannot fail to recognize that the cottage overgrown with
plants is not merely the *occasion* of moral reflections but a

pictorial embodiment of their meaning: the narrative, the moral commentary, and the picture or setting are inseparable. The contradiction between the extreme ordinariness of this picture—composed as it is of common plumes and weeds and spear-grass—and the quantity of moral meaning it is called upon to express gives to the conclusion of the Wanderer's tale an appearance almost of paradox. The depth of his feelings as he contemplates the spear-grass on the wall might well seem—judged by common-sense standards—out of proportion to the cause assigned. Yet the incident does not strike us as improbable. And the reason is that the poetry leaves no room for doubt that the scene contemplated exists inwardly as well as outwardly; we can believe that the plants and weeds are the cause of profound effects in the life of the mind because they are, demonstrably, of the same stuff as the mind. Wordsworth's success here is partly due to his play on the word 'image'. Qua 'picture', the 'image of tranquillity' is as unremarkable as it could well be; qua 'emblem', it records a spiritual experience that is both remarkable and valuable. (Compare the plural meaning of the word in line 69, Book XIII of *The Prelude*, 1805.) The image is 'calm and still', first because it is a faithful picture of the plumes, weeds and spear-grass—and these are still; secondly because it virtually *is* these objects, since it is indistinguishable from them; and finally because it is a copy not only of tranquil external things but of tranquillity itself. (The heart is so calm that its tranquillity might be considered the very emblem of tranquillity.) The syntax strongly implies that it was not merely the weeds etc. but also their image that 'looked so beautiful', as though image and thing were equally distant from the mind contemplating them—and therefore equally objective. In other words the image tends to become, or dissolve into, the thing itself, the object imaged. And the curious but very characteristic use of the word 'Amid', which manages to connote spatial as well as temporal location, also serves to put thing and image on the same footing, by seeming to locate them both amid uneasy thoughts. (There is a similar use of 'amid' a few lines above: '. . . 'mid the calm oblivious tendencies Of Nature, 'mid her plants . . .'.) So it comes about that the poetry acts out the stated meaning; for the lesson the Wanderer has to teach is that 'the forms of things'—of commonplace things—can carry a great weight of moral meaning, and this is precisely what, to the eye of the reader as well as of the Wanderer himself, the form (or image) of the weeds and so on appears to do.

Before he achieved these austerely beautiful lines about the image Wordsworth made 'three different attempts at a reconciling passage for the close of the poem' (de Selincourt: p. 400). Two of them are of interest for the way they spell out the paradox which in the final version has become implicit. It will be enough to look at the first of these.

> The old man ceased: he saw that I was moved.
> From that low bench rising instinctively
> I turned away in weakness, and my heart
> Went back into the tale which he had told,
> And when at last returning from my mind
> I looked around, the cottage and the elms,
> The road, and pathway, and the garden wall
> Which old and loose and mossy o'er the road
> Hung bellying, all appeared, I know not how
> But to some eye within me all appeared
> Colours and forms of a strange discipline.
> The trouble which they sent into my thoughts
> Was sweet, I looked and looked again, and to myself
> I seemed a better and a wiser man.

Wordsworth explicates the paradox with some deliberation:

36

the colours and forms of cottage, elms and so on impress themselves at one and the same time on an outer and an inner eye, so that the forms can only be forms in a double sense.

The Alfoxden Note Book contains a number of fragments that bear upon my theme (they are printed by de Selincourt in an appendix to Volume V); but I shall choose only one for comment—and select the following because of the way it looks forward to *Tintern Abbey*:

> Why is it we feel
> So little for each other, but for this,
> That we with nature have no sympathy,
> Or with such things as have no power to hold
> Articulate language?
> And never for each other shall we feel
> As we may feel, till we have sympathy
> With nature in her forms inanimate,
> With objects such as have no power to hold
> Articulate language. In all forms of things
> There is a mind.

These lines were written at a period when the word 'forms' was coming to have for Wordsworth a persistently ambiguous connotation. But here the ambiguity is not realized; and as a result he is reduced to merely *asserting* his faith that there is a mind 'in all forms of things'. On numerous occasions, and particularly in *Tintern Abbey*, Wordsworth was to demonstrate this faith poetically, the demonstration depending very much on his persuading us that the forms of things are shapes in a human mind as well as the shapes of a landscape. But the 'forms inanimate' of the lines under review show no signs of being of the same stuff as the mind of the observer and remain purely external. So we have to take the 'doctrine' or 'belief' on trust. Still, the fragment is an interesting pointer to *Tintern Abbey* (or rather to a dominant theme of that poem) because mind is declared to be universally present not, simply, in things but in the forms of things.

There is a long passage about forms and their relation to the human heart in the reflective argument referred to above which was deleted from *The Ruined Cottage* and later included in Book IV of *The Excursion*; but here again the 'forms' remain purely objective and the language scarcely rises above the level of rhetoric:

> For, the Man—
> Who, in this spirit, communes with the Forms
> Of nature, who with understanding heart
> Both knows and loves such objects as excite
> No morbid passions, no disquietude,
> No vengeance, and no hatred—needs must feel
> The joy of that pure principle of love
> So deeply, that, unsatisfied with aught
> Less pure and exquisite, he cannot choose
> But seek for objects of a kindred love
> In fellow-natures and a kindred joy.
> Accordingly he by degrees perceives
> His feelings of aversion softened down;
> A holy tenderness pervades his frame.
> His sanity of reason not impaired,
> Say rather, all his thoughts now flowing clear,
> From a clear fountain flowing, he looks round
> And seeks for good; and finds the good he seeks:
> Until abhorrence and contempt are things
> He only knows by name; and, if he hear,
> From other mouths, the language which they speak,

He is compassionate; and has no thought,
No feeling, which can overcome his love.

          And further; by contemplating these Forms
In the relations which they bear to man,
He shall discern, how, through the various means
Which silently they yield, are multiplied
The spiritual presences of absent things.
Trust me, that for the instructed, time will come
When they shall meet no object but may teach
Some acceptable lesson to their minds
Of human suffering, or of human joy.
So shall they learn, while all things speak of man,
Their duties from all forms; and general laws,
And local accidents, shall tend alike
To rouse, to urge; and, with the will, confer
The ability to spread the blessings wide
Of true philanthropy.

Though these lines can hardly be said to get off the ground,
they are worth quoting as a foil to *Tintern Abbey*—which
comes next in order of composition among the poems relevant
to my argument, and calls for special attention.

V

I BEGIN with the second paragraph:

          These beauteous forms,
Through a long absence, have not been to me
As is a landscape to a blind man's eye:

But oft, in lonely rooms, and 'mid the din
Of towns and cities, I have owed to them
In hours of weariness, sensations sweet,
Felt in the blood, and felt along the heart;
And passing even into my purer mind,
With tranquil restoration . . .

The beauteous forms are the external shapes or visible aspects
of cliff, river, wood etc. and also the ideal shapes that have
lived for five years in the memory. By using the word 'forms'
without the word 'colours', its frequent partner (compare
later in this poem: 'the tall rock, The mountain, and the deep
and gloomy wood, Their colours and their forms . . .') Wordsworth has given us at least some encouragement to dwell on
the contours of the landscape in abstraction from the substances
that fill those contours. And we are the more likely to do so
in that 'form' can also mean 'phantom', i.e. something regarded as having shape without substance. Furthermore, since
'landscape' is virtually a synonym here for 'forms', one strand
of meaning runs, 'These forms have not been forms that exist
outwardly but cannot be seen'; and this proposition implies,
'They *have* been forms that exist *inwardly* and *can* be seen'. In
short, we could paraphrase roughly: 'During my long absence
the forms have by no means been blotted out; they have
continued to exist in the mind as a landscape of impressions.'
The effect of course depends on our *not* distinguishing these
different meanings; and in fact the convolutions of tense (quite
apart from anything else) prevent us from doing so. The scene
contemplated is at once substantial and insubstantial, present
and past.

These dubieties of meaning set up a resonance that is felt
through the rest of the paragraph, and indeed through the
rest of the poem. '. . . I have owed to them, In hours of

weariness, sensations sweet . . .'. Does he owe the sensations to the external forms, or to the impressions these forms have left upon the mind, or to both? Apparently to both. For on the one hand 'them' seems to refer back to 'these' forms at present before the eye; so that the sensations may be regarded as sense-impressions, or mental images, owing their origin to the *physical* landscape (i.e. the landscape perceived years before; for his inward eye has not been like the eye of a man who is blind.) And yet the obvious meaning of sensations is 'feelings' (Felt in the blood, and felt along the heart), so that 'them' must refer not only to the outer forms but to the inner ones seen in lonely rooms etc. According to this reading, the object of the process of inward perception is indicated by 'them' and the subjective component of the process by 'sensations'—an inter- pretation that is confirmed by the dictionary: 'Sensation:— . . . An operation of any of the senses . . . a physical "feeling" considered apart from the resulting "perception" of an object' (O.E.D.). But it is surely clear that within the context of the poetry the word cannot be limited to this single or dictionary meaning: the sensations are the feelings by which the memory- images were accompanied but also, though more obscurely, the memory-images themselves. (Compare *The Prelude* 1.661.1805.) The inner forms derive from the outer forms and the sensations from both. In other words rigid distinctions between outer and inner—that is, between sense-image and memory-image, or sense-image and feeling—fall into abey- ance.

A duplicity in the meaning of the word 'sensation' is some- thing we meet with a good deal in eighteenth-century philo- sophy, and like the duplicity in the meaning of 'consciousness' it points to a radical if generally covert awareness (common to philosopher and layman) that sense-perception is a paradox. Lovejoy speaks of 'the curious neglect of many generations of philosophers and psychologists, following Descartes' example, to distinguish between the -ings and the -eds (to adopt an expression of Professor S. Alexander's)—between the terms "sensation", "perception" or "thought" as signifying the event, function or act of sensing, perceiving, thinking, *etc*, and the same terms as signifying the items sensed, perceived or thought.'

This confusion may have been disastrous in philosophy but Wordsworth, who inherited it, turned it to good account.

If the meaning of 'forms' and 'sensations' is plural, so is the meaning of 'sweet', which often makes an appearance in Wordsworth's poetry when his subject is the dissolving of outward image into inward, or substance into spirit. (Compare the passage quoted above, p. 27.) There is an instance further on in the poem, in the lines addressed to Dorothy:

> and, in after years,
> When these wild ecstasies shall be matured
> Into a sober pleasure; when thy mind
> Shall be a mansion for all lovely forms,
> Thy memory be as a dwelling-place
> For all sweet sounds and harmonies; oh! then,
> If solitude, or fear, or pain, or grief,
> Should be thy portion, with what healing thoughts
> Of tender joy wilt thou remember me,
> And these my exhortations!

Here, as on a number of occasions (see for instance the lines quoted on page 36), 'sweet' occurs in a context concerned with memory, healing thoughts and 'forms'. (Since the forms exist at once externally and in the mind, what contains them must have spatial dimensions as well as spiritual; and must be commodious. Hence 'mansion' and 'dwelling-place'. Compare *The Prelude*, 111.362.1850 and *The Pleasures Of The Imagination*, 11.57.1772.) This instance is strictly analogous with the earlier one (line 27). Indeed 'sweet' is a word very appropriate to Wordsworth's purposes. In the phrase 'sensations sweet' it reminds us of the kind of sensation in which the actual *process* of sensing—and therefore the interpenetration of subject and object—is most obvious (sweet musk-roses, sweet odours, sweet savour) and prepares the way for 'purer mind', 'good man's life' and 'acts of kindness'; for sweet also means 'free from taint or corruption'. The paragraph as a whole (lines 22–49) is concerned with a complex of feelings which we come upon again in Book VI of *The Prelude* (Wordsworth is invoking the neighbourhood of Como):

> Like a breeze
> Or sunbeam over your domain I passed
> In motion without pause; but ye have left
> Your beauty with me, a serene accord
> Of forms and colours, passive, yet endowed
> In their submissiveness with power as sweet
> And gracious, almost might I dare to say,
> As virtue is, or goodness; sweet as love,
> Or the remembrance of a generous deed,
> Or mildest visitations of pure thought,
> When God, the giver of all joy, is thanked
> Religiously, in silent blessedness;
> Sweet as this last herself, for such it is.

We accept Wordsworth's assurance that the forms and colours are, ambiguously, passive-and-active, submissive-and-powerful, because the poetry convinces us unawares that the epistemological status of these forms and colours is itself ambiguous. Their passivity is the passivity of the *external* landscape (the traveller passed rapidly over a domain that did not, by asserting its beauty, actively compel him to pause) but it is also the passivity of the images that were left by the landscape on the memory (images that have lain quietly in the mind but for all their non-assertiveness have been a power). The expression 'serene accord' also contributes to the complex of meaning in an equivocal way. The accord is both an aesthetic fact and a moral one, both the harmonious disposition of forms and colours—outside and inside the mind—and the serene and harmonious feelings which these have induced. The forms and colours exert a power as sweet as love because love (at any rate one kind of love), like sense-images, exerts power by yielding ('submissiveness', 'gracious', 'mildest', 'silent') and is active through being undemonstrative.

But I return now to *Tintern Abbey*. I have already suggested with regard to the mystical experience celebrated on two occasions in the poem that nothing is said in these nodal passages different in kind from what is said less explicitly elsewhere. The flashes of insight into an invisible or more ultimate world seem an inevitable consequence of the way substance and spirit are ambiguously and mysteriously implicated in the simplest act of perception. There is a sense in which 'We see into the life of things' at every point of the poem. As here:

> Once again
> Do I behold these steep and lofty cliffs,
> That on a wild secluded scene impress
> Thoughts of more deep seclusion . . .

Though the cliffs are objects of contemplation they cannot be said to belong, in any simple way, to a solid objective world confronting the thoughts of more deep seclusion, intimately involved as these are with the very scene that gives occasion to them. The cliffs 'impress thoughts on . . .' with something

44

of the immediacy and literalness of a craftsman impressing a pattern on wax. And it is almost as though the impressing goes on without the intervention of the observing mind. (Wordsworth would have found indications of the usefulness of the word 'impress' in *The Pleasures Of The Imagination*.) The consequence is that the thoughts take on something of the objectivity of cliffs and secluded scene, and these latter the subjectivity of thoughts. The formula 'Thoughts of . . .' is ambiguous: a possible meaning is that the thoughts are more secluded than the secluded scene. At any rate the thoughts are not only *about* deep seclusion, they are themselves deep and secluded.

In the lines under immediate review a number of words which play an important role in the poem are drawn together for the first time into a complex of meaning; these are 'lofty', 'wild', 'thoughts', 'deep' and (shortly afterwards) 'quiet'. It is surprising how often certain words in *Tintern Abbey* recur, in shifting contexts. There is a kind of mathematical pleasure to be derived from observing how cunningly Wordsworth's meaning is built up through a principle of permutation, the terms that are combined and re-combined being relatively few for the achievement of such elaborate effects. Apart from 'sense', 'thought', 'heart', 'feeling', 'deep', 'nature', 'life', and 'thing', there are a number of other words of a secondary order of importance that are used twice or even three or four times. And yet for the most part the repetitions have the air of being accidental. Coleridge remarked that 'Nature, the prime genial artist, inexhaustible in diverse powers, is equally inexhaustible in forms', and he proceeded to argue, analogically, that the natural genius composes 'with a seeming freedom and a happy spontaneity and yet achieves a most complex and elaborate art'. (I quote in this last instance from the brilliant discussion of the subject by Professor M. H. Abrams, in *The*

45

*Mirror And The Lamp.*) To illustrate his argument Coleridge might well have referred to *Tintern Abbey*, a poem that is more intricately organized than is usually allowed, though its meaning develops and ramifies in what often appears to be a casual way. Can it be 'intended' that the half-line 'And *rolls* through all things' should recall '*rolling* from their mountain springs', in line 3? Do the lines 'Thy memory be as a *dwelling-place* For all sweet sounds and harmonies' point back to 'Whose *dwelling* is the light of setting suns'? For that matter we find earlier in the poem the phrase 'Vagrant *dwellers* in the houseless woods'. Is this a piece of artistic calculation? A reader who notes such connections and 'cross-references' might well seem guilty of mnemonic irrelevance. And yet repetitions of this kind are so numerous that they cannot be ignored; and analysis reveals that the bulk of them are in fact structurally significant.

Here are some further examples:

*murmur:*   With a soft, inland murmur; Not for this Faint I, nor mourn, nor murmur.

*impress:*   impress Thoughts of more deep seclusion; impress With quietness and beauty.

*motion:*   And even the motion of our human blood; A motion and a spirit.

*quiet:*   the quiet of the sky; an eye made quiet; quietness and beauty.

*deep:*   Thoughts of more deep seclusion; the deep power of joy; by the sides of the deep rivers; deep and gloomy wood; a sense sublime Of something far more deeply interfused; with far deeper zeal Of holier love.

*lofty:*   lofty cliffs (twice); lofty thoughts.

*lone:*   where by his fire The Hermit sits alone; the lonely streams; in lonely rooms.

|            |                                                                                                      |
|-----------:|------------------------------------------------------------------------------------------------------|
| *wild:*    | on a wild secluded scene; little lines Of sportive wood run wild; wild eyes (twice); these wild ecstasies. |
| *gleams:*  | gleams of half-extinguished thought; gleams Of past existence.                                       |
| *behold:*  | Once again Do I behold these steep and lofty cliffs; Oh! yet a little while May I behold in thee what I was once; all which we behold Is full of blessings. |
| *lead:*    | In which the affections gently lead us on; wherever nature led; to lead From joy to joy.              |
| *wander:*  | O sylvan Wye! thou wanderer thro' the woods; Nor wilt thou then forget That after many wan-derings.  |
| *world:*   | the weary weight Of all this unintelligible world; the fever of the world; all the mighty world Of eye, and ear. |
| *bless:*   | that blessed mood; that serene and blessed mood; all which we behold Is full of blessings.           |
| *eye:*     | a blind man's eye; an eye made quiet; nor any interest Unborrowed from the eye; wild eyes (twice).   |
| *sublime:* | Of aspect more sublime; a sense sublime.                                                              |
| *heart:*   | Felt in the blood, and felt along the heart; Have hung upon the beatings of my heart; The guide, the guardian of my heart; The language of my former heart; Knowing that Nature never did be-tray The heart that loved her. |
| *language:*| In nature and the language of the sense; The lan-guage of my former heart.                           |
| *harmony:* | an eye made quiet by the power of harmony; Thy memory be as a dwelling-place For all sweet sounds and harmonies. |

47

| light: | Whose dwelling is the light of setting suns; the shooting lights of thy wild eyes. |
| sky: | the quiet of the sky; And the blue sky, and in the mind of man. |
| form(s): | these beauteous forms; Their colours and their forms; for she can so inform The mind that is within us; when thy mind Shall be a mansion for all lovely forms. |
| life: | a good man's life; and become a living soul; the life of things; life and food For future years; the living air; Through all the years of this our life. |

And so on.

The effect of it all is that distinctions between thought and the objects of thought, things and the feelings that things evoke, are (at one level) suspended. For example: the phrase 'lofty thoughts' is not so distant from the earlier phrase 'lofty cliffs' that their occurrence in the same poem cannot produce a faint overtone of meaning; and yet it is sufficiently distant to prevent the emergence of an association of ideas that would be merely ridiculous (viz. 'These cliffs are lofty and so on occasion are my thoughts'). The verbal identity-in-difference (the same adjective applied to two nouns quite diverse apparently in reference) argues quietly for the possibility of a more radical kind of identity. If cliffs and thoughts are both 'lofty'; if the sky and the human eye are alike 'quiet'; the soul and the air both 'living'; if both river and human observer wander; if the light of setting suns is a 'dwelling', and the memory a 'dwelling-place'; if the spirit or presence is 'a motion' and 'our human blood' also felt as 'motion', etc. etc., then it becomes difficult for the reader to sustain without radical qualification a normal, common-sense distinction between the living and the lifeless. Notions of depth, penetration, and seclusion (a soft

48

*in*land murmur, *im*press, *in* the houseless woods, and passing even *into* my purer mind, see *into* the life of things, *in*form the mind that is *within* us) are intricately associated with the notion of height; and with power, joy and quietness. (Even when 'the deep rivers', 'the tall rock' and 'the deep and gloomy wood' are not directly associated with quietness but rather with aching joys and dizzy raptures, the overall mood is still one of quiet reflection: 'That time is past'.) The visionary power—the capacity for exaltations and deep insights—comes into being through the refinement of a more familiar and pedestrian power, a power manifest in everyday acts of sense-perception, where (supposing we are concerned with a scene in nature) thought is impressed deep into the stuff of the landscape and natural objects penetrate deep into the mind. Though the analogy between spiritual and sensory vision is an ancient one ('We see into the life of things') in the context of this poem it has a special force.

It may perhaps be objected that there is nothing unusual or particularly significant about Wordsworth's use of the same words to refer to external objects and the inner life, since the language that human beings employ to express feeling or describe inward events is *necessarily* metaphorical, being built up of analogies drawn from the public world of material things; so that it is inevitable that we should speak of *sharp* pain, *far-reaching* ambition, *deep* thought, and so on. In other words what Wordsworth is doing in *Tintern Abbey* is linguistically interesting but of no ontological significance, and it is not evidence that he is poised between a realistic view of the universe and a subjective. To this objection I would answer first, that I am not claiming that Wordsworth's poetry is directly significant as philosophy; and second, that granted the language of the inner life is unavoidably metaphoric what is important about *Tintern Abbey* is the *patterning* of the metaphors, the close *organisation* of meaning. (Professor J. N. Findlay contributed a very illuminating article on this subject to *Philosophy And Phenomenological Research*, 1948, under the title 'Recommendations Regarding The Language Of Introspection'.)

So what Wordsworth achieves in *Tintern Abbey* is a 'dramatisation of the spiritual', to adopt an expression of Mr. Wimsatt's in *The Verbal Icon*; though the drama is not to be found, primarily, where Mr. Wimsatt finds it. He refers to the poem as a classic instance of the way the Romantics summoned spiritual meaning out of the very surface of nature itself, without resorting to explicit religious or philosophic statement; it is

'a whole pantheistic poem woven of the landscape, where God is not once mentioned. After the "soft inland murmur", the "one green hue", the "wreaths of smoke . . . as . . . Of vagrant dwellers in the houseless woods" (always something just out of sight or beyond definition), it is an easy leap to the "still, sad music of humanity," and

a sense sublime
Of something far more deeply interfused,
Whose dwelling is the light of setting suns.

This poem, written as Wordsworth revisited the banks of a familiar stream, the "sylvan Wye", is the full realization of a poem for which Coleridge and Bowles had drawn slight sketches. In Shelley's "Hymn to Intellectual Beauty" the "awful shadow" of the "unseen Power" is substantiated of moonbeam showers of light behind the "piny mountain", of "mist o'er mountains driven". On the Lake of Geneva in the summer of 1816 Byron, with Shelley the evangelist of Wordsworth at his side, spoke of "a living fragrance from the shore", a "floating whisper on the hill". We remark in each of these examples a dramatisation of the spiritual through the use of the faint, the shifting, the least tangible and most mysterious parts of nature—a poetic counterpart of the several theories of spirit as subtile matter current in the eighteenth century.'

To class Wordsworth, Byron and Shelley together in such a context is somewhat misleading. It is clear enough that the features of the landscape with which Wordsworth is concerned in *Tintern Abbey* are not 'always . . . just out of sight or beyond definition'; it would be sufficient to draw attention to the plots of cottage ground, the hedge-rows and the pastoral farms to prove this. Admittedly certain features of the scene are 'faint' or 'shifting'; but the poem is constructed not so much around the primary metaphors of evanescence and intangibility as around the metaphor of penetration. A good deal of the life or drama in the verse comes from a tension between forms and things: the universal spirit impels both objects ('things') and 'objects of *thought*'. The plots of cottage ground and the orchard-tufts exist both in their own right and as image ('one green hue'). Half-perceived and half-created, the landscape is part of the 'mighty world' and also an inward experience ('the mighty world Of eye, and ear').

If ever a nature-poet earned the right to personify, Wordsworth did in this poem. The ease with which the beauteous forms of the landscape are translated into the inward life of the observer—into sensations sweet, feelings of unremembered pleasure, affections, joy, elevated thoughts—goes a long way towards validating the climactic metamorphosis of the whole natural world into a 'person', in line 122:

> Knowing that Nature never did betray
> The heart that loved her.

For the first time in the poem Nature (spelt with a capital) is personified outright—hypostatized as a large, dim identity immanent in but also transcending the natural scene. And we find the personification completely acceptable. Already convinced that what is physical is by the same token a mental experience, we find it easy to conceive of Nature, simultaneously, as the world of natural objects and a personality— a Goddess with purposes in some measure comprehensible to man. This effect of double exposure has been prepared for by everything that has gone before: i.e. by the 'cross-references' and by the pervasive plurality of meaning already remarked on. To select arbitrarily one of many possible examples, we may note how unobtrusively the 'affections' of line 42 recall the 'sensations' of line 27. The sensations are felt in hours of weariness, the affections when the heavy and the weary weight of all this unintelligible world is lightened; the sensations are felt *along* the heart . . . *passing* even into (the) purer mind . . . (a sense of passage or progression is of the essence of the experience), while the affections lead us *on*; the sensations pass into the mind with *tranquil* restoration, and the affections lead on *gently*. So when we read later:

> 'tis her privilege,
> Through all the years of this our life, to *lead*
> From joy to joy

the leading is inevitably conceived of as at once a guidance from without (we also half-remember '. . . by the sides Of the deep rivers, and the lonely streams, Wherever nature *led*') and an impulse from within (for it is the affections that are leading us on); the two meanings jostle, as it were, for priority of attention. The primary paradox of sense-awareness is so cunningly elaborated in *Tintern Abbey* that it would be difficult to find a better instance of what Mr. Wimsatt has called 'romantic wit'.

## VI

IN the following section I shall endeavour to consolidate my argument. I shall range over the poems freely to show that the conclusion that Wordsworth uses the words 'form', 'shape' and 'image' equivocally has not been arrived at on the evidence of half a dozen cannily selected instances, and that almost anywhere we turn and dip (in the poetry of the great decade, that is) we discover the same feeling for the ambiguity of perception.

The first passage is taken from the 1805 version of *The Prelude*:

>                     Yet in the midst
>     Of these vagaries, with an eye so rich
>     As mine was, through the chance, on me not wasted,
>     Of having been brought up in such a grand
>     And lovely region, I had forms distinct
>     To steady me; these thoughts did oft revolve
>     About some centre palpable, which at once
>     Incited them to motion, and control'd,
>     And whatsoever shape the fit might take,
>     And whensoever it might come, I still
>     At all times had a real solid world
>     Of images about me; . . .

The primary meaning of 'images' here seems to be 'Nature's image-work': the young poet is surrounded by pictures, but real solid pictures. However, given the context, a comparison-and-contrast with *mental* images seems also to be implied: 'the images were pictures, as all images are, including images in the mind; yet they were *not* images in the mind, for they were solid'. As so often in poetry the effect of this denial of a meaning is that the meaning denied begins to assert itself as a positive value, thus: 'The images were solid *and yet* were optical appearances'. Moreover we have learnt a few lines earlier that the 'forms distinct' steadied the mind and the thoughts revolved 'About some centre palpable' as though both thoughts and forms were operating in a space at once mental and physical. When therefore the metaphor of the circle ('*About* some centre . . .') is covertly repeated ('. . . a real solid world Of images *about* me') the reader tends to assume that the relationship between the images and the self, like that between the forms and the thoughts, is not purely external: in other words 'about me' is not interpreted simply as 'outside and independent of me' but also as 'centred upon me' and even perhaps, in some sense, 'dependent upon me'.

Here, from *The Prelude*, is a further example of ingenious double-talk:

> No familiar shapes
> Remained, no pleasant images of trees,
> Of sea or sky, no colours of green fields;
> But huge and mighty forms, that do not live
> Like living men, moved slowly through the mind
> By day, and were a trouble to my dreams.
> Wisdom and Spirit of the universe!
> Thou Soul that art the eternity of thought,

That givest to forms and images a breath
And everlasting motion, not in vain
By day or star-light thus from my first dawn
Of childhood didst thou intertwine for me
The passions that build up our human soul . . .

Shapes, images, forms—our three key terms do a great deal of
work here. Moreover 'shape' has been used shortly before, in
reference to the 'huge peak':

I struck and struck again,
And growing still in stature the grim shape
Towered up between me and the stars . . .

The solidity of the peak is a distinctly qualified solidity, for
'shape', we know, can mean spectre or phantom. (Compare
*Paradise Lost* 11.649,666 ff., and 681. For 'grim' see *P.L.* 11.804;
and also *Fragment Of A Gothic Tale*—de Selincourt's edition,
Volume 1, p. 291.) When we come upon the next usage we
shall not have forgotten the mobility and ambiguous status of
the huge, black peak—the grim shape—and this will pre-
dispose us to find in the familiar shapes or pleasant images a
like mobility, a capacity to be at once there and here, to exist
both outwardly and inwardly. (It was precisely this mobility
that Hobbes denied to the image: '. . . and yet the introducing
of *Species visible* and *intelligible* [which is necessary for the
maintenance of that Opinion] passing to and fro from the
*Object*, is *worse* than any Paradox as being a plain *impossibility*.')
'To remain' can mean both 'to continue in the same state' and
'to be left over—as a residue or trace'. The shapes are, first and
foremost, impressions left on the mind. But 'familiar', taken
in conjunction with the alternative meaning of 'Remained',
suggests that they are also objects in the natural world—well-
known objects that endure: no familiar shapes remained either

inwardly or outwardly. In short the sinister power of the language can largely be traced to an unstated meaning: viz. that the darkness hangs over both the boy's thoughts and the whole visible world. (The 'huge and mighty forms . . . moved slowly through the mind' not only at night but also 'by day'.) The inner chaos has spread outwards and engulfed the entire imagery of nature.

In his invocation to the 'Wisdom and Spirit of the universe' Wordsworth is elaborating and modifying some earlier lines which are to be found in Manuscript V. (de Selincourt publishes them as a footnote.)

> Oh not in vain, ye Beings of the hills,
> And ye that walk the woods and open heaths
> By moon or starlight, thus from my first dawn
> Of childhood, did ye love to intertwine . . .

The rural and pagan charm of these lines gives way to splendour and sublimity in the published version. And it is largely because of the substitution of those 'forms and images' for the 'hills . . . (and) woods and open heaths' of the original that Wordsworth's sudden ascent to the sublime is so easy and convincing. For the 'forms and images' are both configurations in the mind and configurations in the external world; so their presence justifies the appeal to a Spirit diffused widely through time and place and residing, indifferently, in nature or the mind of man. Moreover, because of the preceding lines about the pleasant images and huge and mighty forms, the *mobility* of the natural world is already suggested by the equivocal 'forms and images' before we reach the words 'breath' and 'motion'; and indeed without this equivocation the reality of the Spirit would have been largely a matter of assertion.

Wordsworth's 'imagination'—in the sense of inner vision or 'inward eye'—seems to have been most active when the outward vision was also engaged (despite what the poem 'I wandered lonely . . .' might suggest).

> At length, the dead Man, 'mid that beauteous scene
> Of trees, and hills and water, bolt upright
> Rose with his ghastly face; a spectre shape
> Of terror even! and yet no vulgar fear,
> Young as I was, a Child not nine years old,
> Possess'd me; for my inner eye had seen
> Such sights before, among the shining streams
> Of Fairy land, the Forests of Romance:
> Hence came a spirit hallowing what I saw
> With decoration and ideal grace;
> A dignity, a smoothness, like the works
> Of Grecian Art, and purest Poesy.

This 1805 version is a clear improvement on the lines to be found in MS V:

> Rose with his ghastly face. I might advert
> To numerous accidents in flood or field
> Quarry or moor, or mid the winter snows
> Distresses and disasters, tragic facts
> Of rural history that impressed my mind
> With images to which in following years
> Far other feelings were attached, with forms
> That yet exist with independent life
> And like their archetypes know no decay.

There is a sharp disjunction here of outer and inner—i.e. of tragic facts and impressions on the mind, inward forms and their outward archetypes—and the lines are colourless and flat. In the 1805 version all this gives way to characteristic equivocation: the scene is now both actual and ideal. The word 'scene' itself, in MS V, already implies that the eye is contemplating a picture or image, and this suggests however faintly that the existence of the trees and hills and water is not *merely* objective—a meaning (or intimation of a meaning) that is confirmed in the 1805 version by the introduction of the word 'shape'. Because the child's mind is not confronted by a reality entirely alien to itself—that is, because the anxiety-experience occurs within a scenic context, a realm of shapes as much as things—we easily accept the statement about the transforming power of the 'inner eye' and the assurance that the soul was not debased by terror. (In MS V the record of this incident is followed by the lines that became XI, 258 ff. of *The Prelude*— i.e. the famous passage about the 'spots of time', those moments of high significance when we feel deeply

> that the mind
> Is lord and master, and that outward sense
> Is but the obedient servant of her will.)

The inward streams and forests, and the dead man and beauteous scene, are alike 'sights'—or intervenient images. Incidentally, the comparison of the spectre shape with an artefact is in accordance with Wordsworth's inclination to merge art and nature—his partial equation of natural (or sense) images, ideal (or inward) images, and poetic images:

> On Man, on Nature, and on Human Life,
> Musing in solitude, I oft perceive
> Fair trains of imagery before me rise . . .

or:

> Some lovely Image in the song rose up
> Full-formed, like Venus rising from the sea . . .

58

In the Fenwick note to *Resolution And Independence* he makes the quaint remark: 'The image of the hare I then observed on the ridge of the Fell.'

Scattered up and down the poems are any number of such instances of perception that is simultaneously visual and visionary:

> Sweet Highland Girl, a very shower
> Of beauty is thy earthly dower!
> Twice seven consenting years have shed
> Their utmost bounty on thy head:
> And these grey rocks; that household lawn;
> Those trees, a veil just half withdrawn;
> This fall of water that doth make
> A murmur near the silent lake;
> This little bay; a quiet road
> That holds in shelter thy Abode—
> In truth together do ye seem
> Like something fashioned in a dream;
> Such Forms as from their covert peep
> When earthly cares are laid asleep!
> But, O fair Creature! in the light
> Of common day, so heavenly bright,
> I bless Thee, Vision as thou art,
> I bless thee with a human heart;
> God shield thee to thy latest years!
> Thee, neither know I, nor thy peers;
> And yet my eyes are filled with tears.

The Forms are phantoms and also aspects of the given scene; though visionary, they compose a landscape 'in the light Of common day'. Apart from the line about the trees—'a veil just half withdrawn'—no attempt is made, by an evocation of 'the least tangible and most mysterious parts of nature', to prepare us for the words 'dream' and 'vision'. (I quote again from Mr. Wimsatt's essay.) And in this respect there is an obvious contrast with, say, Collins's *Ode To Evening*, with its 'dying gales', 'time-hallow'd pile', 'dim-discover'd spires' and so on. The grey rocks and household lawn and little bay are as un-mysterious as they could well be. Because, more than anything else, of the play on the word 'Forms', Wordsworth can be at once mysterious here and matter-of-fact, or naturalistic.

And the same comment applies to these lines, though the relevant words here are 'Shape' and 'Image':

> She was a Phantom of delight
> When first she gleamed upon my sight;
> A lovely Apparition, sent
> To be a moment's ornament;
> Her eyes as stars of Twilight fair;
> Like Twilight's, too, her dusky hair;
> But all things else about her drawn
> From May-time and the cheerful Dawn;
> A dancing Shape, an Image gay,
> To haunt, to startle, and way-lay.
>
> I saw her upon nearer view,
> A Spirit, yet a Woman too!
> Her household motions light and free,
> And steps of virgin-liberty;
> A countenance in which did meet
> Sweet records, promises as sweet;
> A Creature not too bright or good
> For human nature's daily food;
> For transient sorrows, simple wiles,
> Praise, blame, love, kisses, tears, and smiles.

And now I see with eye serene
The very pulse of the machine;
A Being breathing thoughtful breath,
A Traveller between life and death;
The reason firm, the temperate will,
Endurance, foresight, strength, and skill;
A perfect Woman, nobly planned,
To warn, to comfort, and command;
And yet a Spirit still, and bright
With something of angelic light.

This little poem is a perfect example of the way Wordsworth will entangle a moral or spiritual theme with ambiguities concerning sense-perception. Like any other sense-image (she gleamed upon my *sight*) the dancing Shape is at once insubstantial and a part of nature. Though impalpable and elusive, she is not *merely* a Phantom or Apparition: she is as real as Twilight and the Dawn. It is largely because of these concealed ambiguities that we modulate so easily from the first stanza to the second (I *saw* her upon nearer view) where the Shape or Image (like other visible images) is discovered to be both spirit and substance. In one way the 'career' of this woman is reminiscent of that of the child in *Ode. Intimations Of Immortality* (where the relating of the life of the spirit to questionings of sense is so much more explicit): at the close of the poem she is more nearly bound to the earth than at the beginning—and yet retains 'something of angelic light'.


The word 'shape' is used ambiguously not only as noun but also as verb:

All things, responsive to the writing, there
Breathed immortality, revolving life,

And greatness still revolving; infinite:
There littleness was not; the least of things
Seemed infinite; and there his spirit shaped
Her prospects, nor did he believe,—he saw.

(*The Excursion*, I)

Or:

By influence habitual to the mind
The mountain's outline and its steady form
Gives a pure grandeur, and its presence shapes
The measure and the prospect of the soul
To majesty; such virtue have the forms
Perennial of the ancient hills . . .

(*The Prelude*, VII)

The mountain gives its grandeur and shapes the soul immediately, just as, in *The Prelude* Book II (170, 1805), the water lies upon the mind directly with a weight of pleasure. No principle of association, no mediation between man and nature, is invoked to explain how nature educates the soul. For that which shapes the outward prospect by the same token shapes the inward. (There is no need to comment here on the words 'outline' and 'form'.)


Wordsworth's poetry often implies, and occasionally claims explicitly, that the feeling attendant upon an act of sense-perception is quite as objective as the things that are sensed. Indeed no poet does more justice to the fact that, as Bosanquet remarked, 'feelings get into objects'. In *The Recluse* he writes:

Joy spreads, and sorrow spreads; and this whole Vale,
Home of untutored Shepherds as it is,
Swarms with sensation, as with gleams of sunshine,

> Shadows or breezes, scents or sounds. Nor deem
> These feelings, though subservient more than ours
> To every day's demand for daily bread,
> And borrowing more their spirit, and their shape
> From self-respecting interests, deem them not
> Unworthy therefore, and unhallowed . . .

The manifest meaning of 'sensation' here is 'feelings' or 'emotions'; but a further, latent meaning is 'sense-perceptions'. We accept the assurance that sensations *qua* feelings exist out there in the Vale along with the gleams of sunshine, the shadows, breezes, scents and sounds, partly because we recognize that where sensations *qua* sense-perceptions are concerned, object so easily becomes subject and subject object. In *The Ruined Cottage* (Volume V, p. 388) we see how this tendency to objectify emotion is associated with the disposition to see nature as a world of forms or shapes as much as a world of things:

> To every natural form, rock, fruit and flower
> Even the loose stones that cover the highway
> He gave a moral life, he saw them feel
> Or linked them to some feeling. In all shapes
> He found a secret and mysterious soul,
> A fragrance and a spirit of strange meaning.

Is it not because Wordsworth is concerned here with natural forms and shapes more than things that he has the confidence to assert that he saw the stones and so on feel? In other words, is it not implied that the forms can feel and the shapes have a soul because they are images, and therefore not alien to the mind? Here is a clearer instance, involving a characteristic use of the verb 'to be':

> the tall rock,
> The mountain, and the deep and gloomy wood,

> Their colours and their forms, were then to me
> An appetite; a feeling and a love . . .

Rock, mountain and wood were not merely the occasion and object of feeling; also—and more mysteriously—they *were* that feeling. At first these natural objects are offered to contemplation as being, unquestionably, solid and material: 'the tall rock, The mountain . . .'. But then the phrase 'their colours and their forms' quietly shifts the reader's attention from things themselves to images of things (we are suddenly aware of the landscape as a scene, with a pattern) and this prepares the way for the subsequent fusion, or partial fusion, of inner and outer, feeling and sensation. If Wordsworth had made the bald, startling assertion that rock, mountain and wood were to him an appetite—that is, if the phrase 'their colours and their forms' had not been inserted where in fact it was inserted—the resultant cancelling of the distinction between inner and outer would have struck the reader as so violent as to be absurd.

It is true that in order to explain the apparent existence of feelings out there in nature Wordsworth often resorts to the common-sense associationist theory which he inherited from the eighteenth century; and in the lines quoted above from *The Ruined Cottage* the words 'he saw them feel' are balanced by 'Or linked them to some feeling'. But he was as ready to believe that feelings are *found* in nature as to believe that they are transferred to nature:

> For me, when my affections first were led
> From kindred, friends, and playmates, to partake
> Love for the human creature's absolute self,
> That noticeable kindliness of heart
> Sprang out of fountains . . .
>
> (*The Prelude*, VIII, 1850)

64

Clearly, his belief in the pervasiveness of feeling is not only arrived at by contemplating the *appearances* of nature (the kindly power that wells up with mysterious impartiality in fountains and the human heart is not known by sense-perception). Nevertheless this faith in the ubiquity of life and spirit is also dependent on knowledge provided by the senses, and is related to Wordsworth's perplexity concerning images or forms. Again and again the poetry demonstrates that joy spreads, and sorrow spreads, because sensations have dimensions that are at once mental and spatial.

I have already touched on the ambiguity of the image as *picture*, but the subject calls for further attention.

> And now with gleams of half-extinguished thought,
> With many recognitions dim and faint,
> And somewhat of a sad perplexity,
> The picture of the mind revives again.

The scene contemplated is a strange blend of outer and inner, present and past. The memory-image comes to life ('revives') both in the sense that it is called to mind and in the sense that it is visibly and tangibly embodied in the landscape at present before the eyes—as though a faded old print were suddenly to acquire not merely colour but substance. Hence the 'perplexity'; for the present picture is vivid, whereas the recollections, or recognitions, are dim and faint.

Eighteenth-century poets, from Pope onwards, showed a fondness for writing of natural scenery in terms of pictorial art, and Wordsworth is certainly indebted to this tradition.

> But who can paint
> Like Nature? Can imagination boast,
> Amid its gay creation, hues like hers?

asks Thomson. But Wordsworth complicates this simple eighteenth-century meaning by suggesting that the fabric on which
the picture is painted, or rather the picture itself, is at once
material and immaterial. (This notion is lurking in Thomson's
lines too, but he makes little poetic capital of it.)

> For oft the Eternal Spirit, He that has
> His life in unimaginable things,
> And he who painting what He is in all
> The visible imagery of all the World
> Is yet apparent chiefly as the Soul
> Of our first sympathies.
>    (Addendum to MS B of *The Ruined Cottage*)

By contrast with the un-imag-inable things the visible imagery
seems solid and earthy. Yet it cannot be wholly so, for it is in
terms of this imagery that the Eternal Spirit paints what He
*is*. The metaphor from painting enables Wordsworth to have
it both ways: the imagery is a manifest creation of pure Spirit,
a scene from the palette of the Eternal Artist; at the same time
it exists, massively, in three dimensions ('all the World'), as we
would expect of a large-scale and well-executed landscape.

If image meant to Wordsworth what I have claimed it to
mean, then it becomes clear why he should have been so
intrigued by reflections in water. Here is an instance from *The
Recluse*:

> —How vast the compass of this theatre,
> Yet nothing to be seen but lovely pomp
> And silent majesty; the birch-tree woods
> Are hung with thousand thousand diamond drops
> Of melted hoar-frost, every tiny knot
> In the bare twigs, each little budding-place
> Cased with its several bead, what myriads there
> Upon one tree, while all the distant grove

That rises to the summit of the steep
Shows like a mountain built of silver light.
See yonder the same pageant, and again
Behold the universal imagery
Inverted, all its sun-bright features touched
As with the varnish, and the gloss of dreams;
Dreamlike the blending also of the whole
Harmonious landscape; all along the shore
The boundary lost, the line invisible
That parts the image from reality;
And the clear hills, as high as they ascend
Heavenward, so piercing deep the lake below.

The 'universal imagery' is nature's image-work; in other words it belongs to the *real* universe of hills, woods and so on. This imagery becomes an *unreal* image by being inverted: 'the line invisible That parts the image from reality'. This second use of image reminds us that all sense-images are reflections and raises faint retrospective doubts about the universal imagery of woods and mountains. Is not this imagery composed of images? And perhaps the solidity of all images, including the most solid-seeming, is questionable. After all, several theatrical metaphors—'theatre', 'pomp', 'shows', 'pageant'—have already laid us open to the suggestion that Nature's show-piece is more surface than substance. If when we are contemplating exceptionally faithful reflections in water 'the line . . . That parts the image from reality' is invisible to us, how much more so is this true of our other—and more normal —visual sensations. It is surely doubts of this kind that determine Wordsworth's double use of 'image' here, as elsewhere it determines his casualness about distinguishing images from things. We recall the lines from *The Prelude* (already quoted) where the comprehensive term 'imagery' includes, in a single tolerant embrace, things themselves, things reflected in water, and things reflected in the mind:

> or the visible scene
> Would enter unawares into his mind,
> With all its solemn imagery, its rocks,
> Its woods, and that uncertain heaven, received
> Into the bosom of the steady lake.

The famous skating episode in *The Prelude* provides further illustration of the fact that Wordsworth was habitually 'perplexed' by the relation of things to their reflections.

> Not seldom from the uproar I retired
> Into a silent bay, or sportively
> Glanced sideway, leaving the tumultuous throng,
> To cut across the reflex of a star
> That fled, and, flying still before me, gleamed
> Upon the glassy plain; and oftentimes,
> When we had given our bodies to the wind,
> And all the shadowy banks on either side
> Came sweeping through the darkness, spinning still
> The rapid line of motion, then at once
> Have I, reclining back upon my heels,
> Stopped short; yet still the solitary cliffs
> Wheeled by me—even as if the earth had rolled
> With visible motion her diurnal round!

It is amusing to watch Wordsworth getting himself out of a difficulty here; for 'reflex' replaces 'image' from the 1805 version. Since 'image' was apt to be identified in his mind with the thing itself as well as with the reflection of it, he must have felt (perhaps unconsciously) that the original version implied, if only dimly, that it was the actual star in the heavens that the skater cut across. And even when the correction has been made the distinction between things and their reflections is still not rigidly preserved. For how can we say that the reflex of the star, as it flies and gleams before the ardent young skater, is less real, less firmly established in the objective world, than the spinning banks or wheeling cliffs? But this is to account for only half the effect of the poetry, for the implicit 'phenomen-alism' is countered by a line of meaning more consonant with common sense. The silent bay and the glassy plain are, after all, stable and substantial enough, while the sonorous final lines (despite 'Wheeled' and 'visible motion') leave us con-vinced that the world is solid and massively real.

Wordsworth takes manifest delight in assuring himself that images have depth. This is partly why he is attracted by the words 'deep' and 'impress', and why he makes such frequent use of metaphors drawn from the art of painting, whose ex-ponents can create a three-dimensional world on a mere sur-face. Depth in a scene was apt to be identified by him with depth of emotional impression, and with spiritual profundity, as *Tintern Abbey* and dozens of passages from *The Prelude* prove; moreover it was a reassuring sign to him that the imagery he was contemplating was not merely an impression on the mind but had solidity. And it was essential to him that images should be solid if they were to be effective vehicles of moral meaning. *Merely* tenuous and dream-like landscapes were of little interest to him. Even the panorama of mist seen from Snowdon, which is an exception among his landscapes, at least *looks* solid. It is the fact that Wordsworth's world of images resists an easy dissolution into spiritual meaning that accounts for that satisfying sense of difficulties met which accompanies our reading of his best poetry.

But I return now to the topic immediately under discussion. Here is a conspicuous instance of imagery that exists in depth:

As one who hangs down-bending from the side
Of a slow-moving boat, upon the breast
Of a still water, solacing himself
With such discoveries as his eye can make
Beneath him in the bottom of the deep,
Sees many beauteous sights—weeds, fishes, flowers,
Grots, pebbles, roots of trees, and fancies more,
Yet often is perplexed and cannot part
The shadow from the substance, rocks and sky,
Mountains and clouds, reflected in the depth
Of the clear flood, from things which there abide
In their true dwelling; now is crossed by gleam
Of his own image, by a sun-beam now,
And wavering motions sent he knows not whence,
Impediments that make his task more sweet;
Such pleasant office have we long pursued
Incumbent o'er the surface of past time
With like success, nor often have appeared
Shapes fairer or less doubtfully discerned
Than these to which the Tale, indulgent Friend!
Would now direct thy notice. Yet in spite
Of pleasure won, and knowledge not withheld,
There was an inner falling off—I loved,
Loved deeply all that had been loved before,
More deeply even than ever: but a swarm
Of heady schemes jostling each other, gawds,
And feast and dance, and public revelry,
And sports and games (too grateful in themselves,
Yet in themselves less grateful, I believe,
Than as they were a badge glossy and fresh

Of manliness and freedom) all conspired
To lure my mind from firm habitual quest
Of feeding pleasures, to depress the zeal
And damp those yearnings which had once been mine—
A wild, unworldly-minded youth, given up
To his own eager thoughts. It would demand
Some skill, and longer time than may be spared,
To paint these vanities, and how they wrought
In haunts where they, till now, had been unknown.
It seemed the very garments that I wore
Preyed on my strength, and stopped the quiet stream
Of self-forgetfulness.

The act of visual perception is emblematised here as a process
of penetration and discovery: what is at first a mere surface
('the breast of a still water') soon becomes a varied, three-
dimensional landscape—weeds, fishes, flowers, grots, pebbles,
roots of trees. The difficulty the observer has in distinguishing
substance from reflection only improves the analogy with
visual perception in general, as does the fact that the under-
water world explored by the eye turns out to be at once the
world of sense and the world of memory. As the paragraph
progresses it becomes increasingly difficult to preserve the
distinctions between the surface of the mind, the surface of the
lake and 'the surface of past time'; or between sensory, mnemonic and moral perception. The youthful Wordsworth, we
are assured, loved *deeply*, though distracted by the gawds and
vanities of the world. And because this assurance follows so
closely upon the elaborate picture of what can be descried in
the depths of the lake, 'I loved, loved deeply' becomes equated
in the imagination with the meaning 'I saw deeply'. The quest
for reality, or real things, is both a movement in depth and a
sustained endeavour to part the solid from the illusory; and it

brings pleasure. (Compare 'pleasant office', 'pleasure won, and knowledge not withheld', 'feeding pleasures'.) What lured the young Wordsworth from the quest was a swarm of heady schemes, the equivalent of the deceptive reflections, 'impediments' and 'wavering motions' that hindered the observer in the boat. The 'inner falling off' entailed a foregoing—or partial foregoing—of the habit of steady contemplation. This surely is the moral discovery that the poetry makes, and the discovery is clinched at the end of the paragraph when the cardinal Wordsworthian virtue of self-forgetfulness is imaged as a stream. If we forget ourselves—the image implies—we are the more likely to perceive deeply.

A comparable passage is the description of the Calenture in *The Brothers*, where the mariner who in his heart is half a shepherd has a vision of his homeland which is at once a penetrating visual perception and the acknowledgement of a deep, heart-felt truth.

> and, when the regular wind
> Between the tropics filled the steady sail,
> And blew with the same breath through days and weeks,
> Lengthening invisibly its weary line
> Along the cloudless Main, he, in those hours
> Of tiresome indolence, would often hang
> Over the vessel's side, and gaze and gaze;
> And, while the broad blue wave and sparkling foam
> Flashed round him images and hues that wrought
> In union with the employment of his heart,
> He, thus by feverish passion overcome,
> Even with the organs of his bodily eye,
> Below him, in the bosom of the deep,
> Saw mountains; saw the forms of sheep that grazed
> On verdant hills—with dwellings among trees,

And shepherds clad in the same country grey
Which he himself had worn.

The images and hues belong out there in nature, with the
broad blue wave and sparkling foam, but also seem detached
from these, as though they were closer to the mind observing
than to the things observed (Flashed round him; wrought In
union with). Because the mariner is gazing at images or forms
(forms of sheep) as much as things, we easily accept the implication that what he sees down there in the ocean exists deep
in his own mind.


In discussing *Tintern Abbey* I observed in passing that Wordsworth tended to attribute to sense-images and memory-images
the same degree of materiality. This point has an important
bearing on my argument; for the fact that sense and memory
can become so 'indistinguishably mixed' in his poetry bears
further witness to the equivocal solidity of Wordsworth's
real, solid world of images. The paragraph already quoted
from *The Ruined Cottage* (page 29) illustrates what I mean. By
the time the reader has reached

> With these impressions would he still compare
> All his ideal stores, thoughts, shapes, and forms

he is finding it very difficult to distinguish between images
that live in the memory and images impressed on the sense.
(In the 1814 edition of *The Excursion* 'ideal stores' becomes
'remembrances'.) Indeed the word 'impress' or 'impression'—
particularly in association with 'deep'—nearly always points
in Wordsworth's poetry to an interesting confusion or interpenetration of inner and outer. ('Impress' had already been
linked with 'deep' and with 'forms' in *The Pleasures Of The*

F                                    73

*Imagination*.) I have commented on '. . . impress Thoughts of more deep seclusion', in *Tintern Abbey*, so there is no need to say anything further about '. . . and deep feelings had impressed So vividly great objects' in the passage under review from *The Excursion* (1814); and no need to linger over the fact that 'shapes and forms' are placed on a footing with remembrances and thoughts. Generally speaking, when Wordsworth's subject is his recollections of a landscape there is little to show that these recollections are less solid, any less part of the material world, than the outward scene—rocks, trees, cliffs, their forms and shapes.

To support this assertion I have selected, out of many possible examples, this from his major poem of recollection:

> Thus, often in those fits of vulgar joy
> Which, through all seasons, on a child's pursuits
> Are prompt attendants, 'mid that giddy bliss
> Which, like a tempest, works along the blood
> And is forgotten; even then I felt
> Gleams like the flashing of a shield; the earth
> And common face of Nature spoke to me
> Rememberable things; sometimes, 'tis true,
> By chance collisions and quaint accidents
> Like those ill-sorted unions, work suppos'd
> Of evil-minded fairies, yet not vain
> Nor profitless, if haply they impress'd
> Collateral objects and appearances,
> Albeit lifeless then, and doom'd to sleep
> Until maturer seasons call'd them forth
> To impregnate and to elevate the mind.
> —And if the vulgar joy by its own weight
> Wearied itself out of the memory,
> The scenes which were a witness of that joy

Remained, in their substantial lineaments
Depicted on the brain, and to the eye
Were visible, a daily sight; and thus
By the impressive discipline of fear,
By pleasure and repeated happiness,
So frequently repeated, and by force
Of obscure feelings representative
Of joys that were forgotten, these same scenes,
So beauteous and majestic in themselves,
Though yet the day was distant, did at length
Become habitually dear, and all
Their hues and forms were by invisible links
Allied to the affections.

The passage contains illustrations of everything that has been said so far in these pages. There is the paradoxical locution 'substantial lineaments' and the association of 'lineaments' and 'joy' with 'weight'. Then there is the plural significance of 'Remained' and 'forms', the equivocation introduced by the word 'impress'd' (i.e. the uncertainty as to whether it is the 'collateral objects' themselves or merely their 'appearances' that are impressed on the mind) and the ambiguity involved in the use of a metaphor from painting (i.e. the doubt as to whether it is actual substantial scenes that are visible to the eye or their lineaments 'depicted' on the brain). Finally—a persistent motif from beginning to end—there is the blending of sensation with recollection and of the present with the past and future. A sub-implication of the poetry is that the reason why it is difficult to distinguish between sense-perception and perception-in-the-memory is that in each case what is perceived is an image or images, so that mental experience, present and past, forms a continuum.

If feelings may be said to 'get into' Wordsworth's landscapes so also may dreams. As Mr. John Jones observes in his book *The Egotistical Sublime*:

> 'Wordsworth describes the condition of insight as a kind of alert day-dream, an inclusive state, like that of the Leech-Gatherer, embracing waking life, and sleep and death.'

Indeed whenever the contradictions in visual perception become, explicitly or implicitly, the subject of Wordsworth's verse, he is apt at some point in his evocation of the landscape to revert to the analogy of the dream.

> Oft in these moments such a holy calm
> Would overspread my soul, that bodily eyes
> Were utterly forgotten, and what I saw
> Appeared like something in myself, a dream,
> A prospect in the mind.

Or:

> . . . and on their pictured lines
> Intensely brooded, even till they acquired
> The liveliness of dreams.

de Selincourt's note on these lines runs:

> 'It is generally stated that the images of dreams are vague and indistinct and lack colour. Wordsworth's experience was the opposite.'

There is any amount of indirect evidence to support this comment: so much indeed that one is tempted to believe that Prospero's words to Ferdinand and Miranda after the masque had for Wordsworth a special appeal. Spirits—thin air—baseless fabric of this vision—the great globe itself—insubstantial pageant—such stuff As dreams are made on—rounded with a sleep: here is a constellation of meanings for which it is not at all difficult to supply Wordsworthian equivalents. Compare for instance the lines from *The Recluse* quoted above: 'See yonder the same *pageant*, and again behold the *universal imagery* . . . touched As with the varnish and the gloss of *dreams*'; or the 'unimaginable sight' described in the Second Book of *The Excursion*; or lines 63–4 in Book XIV of *The Prelude*: 'When into air had partially dissolved That vision, given to spirits of the night'.

The association of dreaming with sense-perception and visionary insight in *Ode. Intimations Of Immortality*—

> Whither is fled the visionary gleam?
> Where is it now, the glory and the dream?

—is too obvious to warrant comment. But it is worth pausing to remark on the analogous association between vision, sense-perception and sleep:

> The cataracts blow their trumpets from the steep;
> No more shall grief of mine the season wrong;
> I hear the Echoes through the mountains throng,
> The Winds come to me from the fields of sleep,
>     And all the earth is gay.

We might paraphrase the fourth line as follows: 'The winds come to me from fields where they have been asleep', or 'The winds are fresh, as after an invigorating sleep in the fields'. For given the immediate context it is difficult not to suppose that the fields are, literally, fields in the vicinity—no less accessible than the cataracts and mountains. On the other hand 'fields of sleep' is, on the face of it, a phrase that fairly cries out to be understood figuratively; so that 'domain of sleep and dreams' might be a more satisfying interpretation—or at any rate an equally satisfying one. The winds come to the poet both from the neighbouring fields and from the dream-fields of childhood—the meadow(s), say, of line 1. The child's perceptions are dream-perceptions ('The glory and the freshness of a dream'.) He is born into sleep; and his dreams are at once visions and sensations. The fields of sleep on this reading are fields-as-they-are-perceived-in-sleep, or fields-invested-with-the-glory-of-sleep. (Frank Kermode comments: 'The basic meaning, I suggest, is "sleep, or inactivity—a fallow period—has refreshed me; out of it blows the wind [of inspiration: as in the opening lines of *The Prelude*]" . . . Basically, the wind is a mental or psychological phenomenon; the wavering between objective description and a sort of allegory of the mental condition probably starts in the previous line, and is justified by the one before that, with the conceit of his grief "wronging" the season.' Professor Abrams has an article on this outward-wind/inward-inspiration ambiguity, entitled 'The Correspondent Breeze: A Romantic Metaphor', in *The Kenyon Review*, Vol. XIX, No. 1.) The child's capacity to perceive vividly while sleeping or, alternatively, to dream while waking can be recovered partially by the grown man, as the image under consideration itself witnesses. If the reader is convinced that the thought of grief has been banished, what convinces him is not so much the explicit assurance that a timely utterance gave that thought relief as the evocation of power and mystery in the passage quoted.

In fact the dream-like vividness and splendour which according to the *Ode* have departed from objects of sight are recovered again and again in the poetry, through the image.

> Oh! then the calm
> And dead still water lay upon my mind
> Even with a weight of pleasure, and the sky
> Never before so beautiful, sank down
> Into my heart, and held me like a dream.

Or:

> This fall of water that doth make
> A murmur near the silent lake;
> This little bay; a quiet road
> That holds in shelter thy Abode—
> In truth together do ye seem
> Like something fashioned in a dream;
> Such Forms as from their covert peep
> When earthly cares are laid asleep!

Or:

> And the whole body of the Man did seem
> Like one whom I had met with in a dream.

It is relevant to remember to what extent Wordsworth's poetry was nourished by the English empirical tradition; for his close association of sensing and dreaming reminds us of Hobbes (*Human Nature*, Chapter 3):

> '*Imagination* being (to define it) *conception remaining and by little and little decaying from and after the act of sense.*
>
> But when *present* Sense is *not*, as in *sleep*, then the *Imagination* remaining after Sense (when there be many) as in Dreams, are *not obscure*, but *strong* and *clear*, as in Sense it self . . .'

From the sheer fact that sense-images are at once solid and ideal Wordsworth passes again and again to the conclusion that we are immortal, and that 'the grief That passing shows of Being leave behind . . . (can) maintain, Nowhere, dominion o'er the enlightened spirit.' Discussing *Ode. Intimations Of Immortality* in a letter to Mrs. Clarkson (Dec. 1814) he writes:

> 'The poem rests entirely upon two recollections of child-

hood, one that of a splendour in the objects of sense which is passed away, and the other an indisposition to bend to the law of death as applying to our particular case.'

On the evidence of Wordsworth's major poems we are justified in assuming that these two recollections were involved intimately with each other. And indeed he himself observes, in the Fenwick note, that it was with a feeling 'congenial' to his sense of the indomitableness of the spirit within him that he 'was often unable to think of external things as having external existence.' That word 'congenial' is amply glossed by the poetry, where Wordsworth's moral concern is so very often inextricable from his pre-occupation with the status of sense-images.

A case in point is the description of the prospect from Snowdon in the last book of *The Prelude*:

> A hundred hills their dusky backs upheaved
> All over this still ocean; and beyond,
> Far, far beyond, the solid vapours stretched,
> In headlands, tongues, and promontory shapes,
> Into the main Atlantic.

Though Wordsworth clearly states that this moonlit panorama seemed to him a type or emblem of the imaginative mind ('a mind That feeds upon infinity'), he also suggests obliquely that it was an emblem of the whole visible world, the real solid world of images. Like that world it is both solid and tenuous, and therefore (so runs the logic of his faith) mind-dependent, and informed with spirit.

The manner in which the moonlight modifies what it shines upon brings to mind some phrases of Coleridge's at the beginning of Chapter XIV of *Biographia Literaria*:

'During the first year that Mr. Wordsworth and I were

80

neighbours, our conversations turned frequently on the two cardinal points of poetry, the power of exciting the sympathy of the reader by a faithful adherence to the truth of nature, and the power of giving the interest of novelty by the modifying colors of imagination. The sudden charm which accidents of light and shade, which moonlight or sunset diffused over a known and familiar landscape, appeared to represent the practicability of combining both.'

The poet who both adheres to the truth of nature and modifies natural objects with the colours of imagination will inevitably deal in images rather than things; but in real solid images—not in ideas, or (in Coleridge's language) phantoms. The panorama of mist seemed to Wordsworth an impressive and satisfying emblem because it displayed so emphatically the plasticity of nature while at the same time adhering to the *truth* of nature, by doing justice to its solidity and faithfully rendering its contours. (The scene is solid-*looking*, and this is all that is required of it *qua* emblem.)

above all
> One function of such mind had Nature there
> Exhibited by putting forth, and that
> With circumstance most awful and sublime,
> That domination which she oftentimes
> Exerts upon the outward face of things,
> So moulds them, and endues, abstracts, combines,
> Or by abrupt and unhabitual influence
> Doth make one object so impress itself
> Upon all others, and pervade them so
> That even the grossest minds must see and hear
> And cannot chuse but feel.

(1805)

Although Wordsworth speaks of one *object* impressing itself upon and pervading all others, it is strongly suggested that the material which Nature is working upon is not so much objects or things as the forms or 'outward face' of things. ('Impress', we have noticed, is a word that comes readily to Wordsworth when he is describing how in an act of perception the mind is invaded by what it perceives.) The domination that Nature exerts is a kind of perception, and the moulding and impressing a kind of image-making.

The manner in which Wordsworth preserves the balance here between the materiality of Nature and its malleability invites comparison with Coleridge's assertion about the function of the secondary Imagination, which

'. . . dissolves, diffuses, dissipates, in order to re-create: or where this process is rendered impossible, yet still at all events it struggles to idealize and to unify. It is essentially *vital*, even as all objects (*as* objects) are essentially fixed and dead.'

In an important article on 'Coleridge's "True And Original Realism" ' in *The Durham University Journal* of March 1961, Mr. Nicholas Brooke has shown that it is not objects as such (i.e. things) that the secondary Imagination dissolves—as Richards, Willey and others have assumed.

'The theory of perception, of imaginative activity, that I have discussed (viz. Coleridge's), is of a coalescence between self and object in which *both* must be assumed to exist. In that theory one cannot speak of "dissolving" the object, because that reduces the object to a phantom, something which does not exist. The confusion is kept alive in the popularity of chemical metaphors for imagination: you can "dissolve" iron (by melting it) and the resultant liquid will "mix" with some other liquids apparently unlike it in kind. But this process is not much use to poetry: it may be that in thinking of iron as cold and hard we are mistaking its nature; but until we understand it better, those remain its perceived, imaginative qualities. And when we speak of a heart of iron we are not linking "heart" and "iron" by the illusion that blood will mix with molten metal: iron functions there precisely because of its unmeltability, its objective *unlikeness* to heart (warmth, blood, adaptability, unreliability, etc.—the emotional character of man rather than the physical organ). In other words, the imaginative force of iron in that phrase depends just on its *not* being dissolved.

So what, if anything, *has* been "dissolved, diffused and dissipated" if it is not the objects themselves? . . . (It) is the *deadness* of dull response, the attenuated cloud that obscures perception; and it is also the *fixity* of relationships in time and space—the fixity of fact that keeps iron in the grate, or for John Gabriel Borkman locked in mountains of stone, utterly distinct from the hearts of men. It is that apparently fixed disjunction which is dissolved: the iron-ness of iron is not changed at all. The "essential nature" of objects is *not* changed; but it is diffused and dissipated over experience from which it is normally regarded as disjunct. If that is not so, there is no meaning in language whatever; we would not be talking about objects, but abstractions, and the words will be found ultimately to be labels, not words at all. That is a condition of insanity, but not of Imagination. Imagination cannot, in its nature as perception, be arbitrary: the objects it deals with must *be* objects.'

Though Wordsworth's prose pronouncements on the subject of imagination and its relation to fancy were repudiated in the *Biographia* very vigorously, there is no reason to suppose that

Coleridge was likely to have been dissatisfied with the meta-phoric or symbolic treatment of the theme in *The Prelude*. For the panorama of solid vapours is a cogent emblem of the operation of perception or imagination as Coleridge under-stood it: we are made vividly aware of the transforming or modifying power of imagination ('moulds', 'combines', 'per-vades') without being required to believe that imaginative activity changes the nature of objects themselves. It is, after all, a *scene* that the moonlight transforms.

The creative energy of Wordsworth's imaginative elect is a refinement of the energy present in any act of perception; and in the 1850 version he speaks of

                              a mind sustained
        By recognitions of transcendent power,
        In sense conducting to ideal form,
        In soul of more than mortal privilege.

The elect

                        build up greatest things
        From least suggestions; ever on the watch,
        Willing to work and to be wrought upon,
        They need not extraordinary calls
        To rouse them; in a world of life they live,
        By sensible impressions not enthralled,
        But by their quickening impulse made more prompt
        To hold fit converse with the spiritual world,
        And with the generations of mankind
        Spread over time, past, present, and to come,
        Age after age, till Time shall be no more.
        Such minds are truly from the Deity,
        For they are Powers; and hence the highest bliss
        That flesh can know is theirs—the consciousness

Of Whom they are, habitually infused
Through every image and through every thought,
And all affections by communion raised
From earth to heaven, from human to divine . . .

The consciousness that is *infused* through every image clearly recalls the object that impresses itself upon all others and pervades them; so that 'image' here easily takes on an equivocal meaning. Consciousness is infused through images, and 'spirit' through 'flesh', because images or sensible impressions from their very inception belong to nature and yet are of the same stuff as the mind. Mere flesh can know 'the highest bliss' (a time-worn theological paradox) because the most exalted operations of the soul are latent in ordinary sense-perception. The very material out of which the visible world is composed argues for the possibility of a ready commerce between sense and ideal form, the human and divine.

To appreciate the function of the image in Wordsworth's poetry is to understand better why he could so frequently extract pleasure from experiences—or the recollection of experiences—that were painful. It is the image of tranquillity conveyed by the plumes and weeds and spear-grass that gives the poet strength to face the anguish of Margaret's history ('I turned And walked along my road in happiness'); and the image of the leech-gatherer (an intervenient image—a kind of dream-image as well as sensation) so fortifies him that the sense of solitude and anxiety by which he had previously been haunted ceases to dismay. In his loneliness and grotesqueness and spectral dignity the old man at once embodies and allays the poet's anxieties. And this is what we learn to expect of the Wordsworthian image, which is apt to be both disturbing and reassuring. A spectre of the mind—a 'spectre shape Of terror' —suddenly confronts the observer as an object in the given world; and the experience exalts while it disturbs, or terrifies. Usually the exaltation comes in the process of recollection. It is in later life that the blank misgivings of a creature moving about in world's not realized cause the poet to raise 'The song of thanks and praise'. In the same way the child's vision of 'unknown modes of being' is alarming at the time but later exhilarating and consoling. The account of the anxiety-experience here leads directly into an ecstatic apostrophising of the Wisdom and Spirit of the Universe. For such experiences prove that our rigid, everyday distinctions between mind and nature are in part illusory. (Or there are these lines from the Preface to *The Excursion*, where the fear is somewhat distanced, and the note of triumph—due in some measure at any rate to uncertainty as to what is inward and what outward—is justified for the most part indirectly, through insistence on the *spaciousness* of the human mind:

> Not Chaos, not
> The darkest pit of lowest Erebus,
> Nor aught of blinder vacancy, scooped out
> By help of dreams—can breed such fear and awe
> As fall upon us often when we look
> Into our Minds, into the Mind of Man—
> My haunt, and the main region of my song.)

Joy, then, is the normal accompaniment in Wordsworth's poetry of 'fear and awe', though no doubt it was rarely blended with these emotions in the original experience. The Wisdom and Spirit of the Universe, that gives to forms and images a breath and everlasting motion, sanctifies

> Both pain and fear, until we recognize
> A grandeur in the beatings of the heart.

86

So images not only provide the poet with the courage to face his spectres; they enable him actually to rejoice in those spectres. Images are a frequent source of anxiety, but also an ultimate source of consolation.


## VII

BUT it would be misleading to suggest that, even in the poetry of the great decade, Wordsworth is always wholly successful in effecting a transition between image and moral reflection (consolatory or joyous); and in order to present a more balanced account of his achievement in this respect I shall devote some attention to *Ode. Intimations Of Immortality*, his most celebrated statement about the bearing that questionings of sense have on the life of the spirit. It is a statement whose impressiveness and beauty are marred by uncertainty of tone, and even a kind of dishonesty.


In the letter that he wrote to Mrs. Clarkson about the *Ode*, Wordsworth remarked after the sentence already quoted (page 51):

'A Reader who has not a vivid recollection of these feelings having existed in his mind cannot understand the poem.'

Wordsworth is mistaken here. The important point about the *Ode* is not that you cannot understand it unless you have similar recollections, but, much more deviously, that the poem rearranges you so that you *seem* to have had the recollections for all poetic purposes. Indeed, if a reader fails to understand the poem or be persuaded by its argument, it will almost certainly not be because the stanzas about the lost splendour and obstinate questionings fail to strike in him a responsive note, but because the poetry does not 'prove' with the necessary rigour that these childhood experiences are significantly related to the moral strength, or philosophic mind, of the adult. For all its brilliance (I shall try to show) the *Ode* is broken-backed.

In his essay on *Wordsworth And Byron* Swinburne drew attention to the crude abruptness of the transition in mood in Stanza IV—

> I hear, I hear, with joy I hear!
> —But there's a Tree, of many, one,
> A single Field which I have looked upon

—and many readers must have felt the instability of tone not only here but in the greater part of the poem. In this same stanza for instance we come upon the lines:

> My heart is at your festival
> My head hath its coronal,
> The fulness of your bliss, I feel—I feel it all.

If the poet can feel with such intensity, with such a plenitude of joy, what, we wonder, can he be said to have lost? The answer that the poem ostensibly supplies is that though the visionary gleam has gone this does not mean that no capacity for joy remains. In Stanzas III and IV there is, in fact, a predominance of joy, and Stanzas X and XI teach us the reason for it. And yet the more we examine these final stanzas the less likely we are to be completely satisfied by them; for they seem to quarrel very seriously with Stanzas V to IX.

88

Wordsworth assures us that he yet feels the might of Nature (though with an acquired sobriety) in his 'heart of hearts'. But how can he, when the grown man's power to respond to the influence of Nature is so meagre? For we recall:

> O joy! that in our embers
> Is something that doth live.

Granted that a living glow remains it is chilling to be told that the man is to the child as embers to the fire. And we are certainly not persuaded that age has its distinctive joys and powers as well as childhood and youth when we learn that it is a prison-house, and that while the youth is attended by the vision

> At length the Man perceives it die away,
> And fade into the light of common day.

In his address on *Leslie Stephen and Matthew Arnold as Critics of Wordsworth* Dover Wilson indignantly rejected G. K. Chesterton's view that these lines are 'blasphemous':

'As if Wordsworth did not spend a whole life-time in hymning just that light of common day which Chesterton, taking the passage out of its context and ignoring even the conclusion of the Ode itself, vainly imagines that he despises. This and not
> The light that never was, on sea or land
was what Wordsworth lived by and for.'

Dover Wilson could certainly find, outside the *Ode*, lines in which the word 'common' has the kind of force he indicates.

> Long have I loved what I behold,
> The night that calms, the day that cheers;
> The common growth of mother-earth

Suffices me—her tears, her mirth,
Her humblest mirth and tears.

But it is by no means clear that 'common' bears a similar favourable connotation in the *Ode*. The imposed meaning of the stanza as a whole (but especially the discouraging phrase 'Shades of the prison-house') forces us to interpret the word in a pejorative sense, though probably Wordsworth intended it to mean nothing more forceful than 'ordinary'. The glory fades; and it is difficult not to feel at this point that what remains is a burden to the heart.

These discrepancies have worried a number of commentators. In *William Wordsworth: His Mind And Art* Beatty argued that, in effect, the *Ode* divides into two distinct poems, 'stanzas I–IV and IX–XI forming a self-consistent poem founded solely on the three ages, and stanzas V–IX a complete intercalary poem on the glory of the child and his derivation from afar, more idealistic and less optimistic than earlier statements.' Stanza IX, he considers, is common to both poems. But even this drastic surgery will not save the *Ode* (or rather the poem formed by its beginning and end) since Stanzas IX and X also refuse to cohere satisfactorily. For if we ask how precisely the 'truths that wake, To perish never' live on into manhood, how the visionary power of the child merges into that of the adult, we find the answer (179–90) confusing.

What though the radiance which was once so bright
Be now for ever taken from my sight,
    Though nothing can bring back the hour
Of splendour in the grass, of glory in the flower
        We will grieve not, rather find
        Strength in what remains behind;
        In the primal sympathy
        Which having been must ever be;

> In the soothing thoughts that spring
> Out of human suffering;
> In the faith that looks through death,
> In years that bring the philosophic mind.

What exactly does Wordsworth mean by 'Strength in what remains behind'? Does he mean 'Strength in what *still lives on* from childhood'? or 'Strength in what we have acquired *since* childhood; Strength in what, despite the loss of childhood, is *yet to come*'? The former would seem, to begin with, to be the more obvious interpretation—until we come to lines 184-5, which can only be interpreted in the second sense, for the 'soothing thoughts' are clearly not inherited from the past; they come with maturity and suffering. This is the first mention in the poem of a specifically adult source of moral strength and it serves to pull the reader up. For though it is made clear in Stanza IX that the 'first affections' remain throughout life a source of power, it is not suggested there that the grown man, building on the firm foundation of childhood, goes from strength to strength, but rather that he draws his strength, quite simply, from the past, living altogether on the steady (or is it diminishing?) capital which the past has bequeathed him:

> Hence in a season of calm weather
> Though inland far we be . . .

The nostalgia here, the backward look at the sea from the continent of human life, does little to prepare us for lines 184-5—'We will grieve not . . .'—which might well come upon the reader with some effect of abruptness. However most readers will interpret 'remains behind', simultaneously, in both of its possible senses, and so will find themselves as they read the lines that follow accepting (though with a vague sense of something being wrong) both the pessimism and the opti-

91

mism, both the nostalgia and the stoicism, both the sense of irreparable loss and the sense of abiding consolation. And line 187 will add the final touch of ambiguity: for while at first sight we might suppose that the philosophic mind belongs exclusively to manhood ('*years* that bring . . .'), and is a substitute for strength peculiar to the child, yet echoes from Stanza VIII force us to deepen this interpretation. 'Philosophic' means, primarily, morally wise, and stoic: man achieves serenity through suffering. But in addition the word points back dimly to 'Thou best philosopher'. The philosophic mind is also the idealizing mind, and looks through death, perhaps, because it refuses to accept as final the given, material world.

It is only by means of these ambiguities that Wordsworth has reconciled in some measure the warring contradictions in the poem. Up to a point the ambiguity is justified, for after all the poetry has in some sense established a continuity between child and man: 'O joy that in our embers . . .'. But the poem becomes dishonest at the point where it takes for granted a closer bond between man and child than it creates. There is no real connection established between the philosophic, *qua* stoic, mind of the man and the child's questionings and blank misgivings; and therefore only the flimsiest of bridges between the nostalgia of the ninth stanza and the soothing sublimities of the eleventh. (Trilling's defence of the *Ode* in *The Liberal Imagination*, though illuminating in some ways, is substantially unconvincing precisely because he fails to take this kind of incoherence into account.) In short, the poetry of consolation does not bear any very intimate relation to the poetry of loss. The fact that the serenity of the final lines is not so much achieved by the poem as ingeniously added to it suggests that the philosophic mind has not mastered the grief but rather come to live side by side with it.

92

But if Wordsworth is not altogether persuasive in the *Ode* it must be added that this case is an exception: his endeavour to make consoling and ennobling poetry out of the image is characteristically successful, as in *The Ruined Cottage*, in *Tintern Abbey*, and again and again in *The Prelude*—to mention only the most compelling instances.

## VIII

IN this concluding section I shall do something to draw the threads of my argument together; and I begin by noting a curious omission in the tabulation of the various meanings of 'image' and 'imagery' in the O.E.D. Here, for ease of reference, is the list of definitions under 'image', with examples where relevant:

1. An artificial imitation or representation of the external form of any object, especially of a person. (a) A statue, effigy, sculptured figure. . . . (b) (Less usually) A likeness, portrait, picture, carving, or the like. (c) Applied to the constellations as figures . . .

2. An optical appearance or counterpart of an object, such as is produced by rays of light either reflected as from a mirror, refracted as through a lens, or falling on a surface after passing through a small aperture. W. Fulke (1640): Appearing as though there were many Sunnes, whereas indeed there is but one, and all the rest are images. Hobbes (*Leviathan*, 1651): From gazing upon the Sun, the impression leaves an image of the Sun before our eyes a long time after. Cowper: Nor Ouse on his bosom their image receives . . .

3. (Abstractly) Appearance, form; semblance, likeness .
(b) A visible appearance, a figure, an apparition. Dryden: The slipp'ry God . . . various Forms assume, to cheat thy sight; And with vain Images of Beasts affright.

4. A counterpart, copy . . .; a symbol, emblem . . .; a type, typical example . . .

5. A mental representation of something (especially a visible object) not by direct perception, but by memory or imagination; a mental picture or impression; an idea, conception ME. Mrs. Radcliffe: She endeavoured to dismiss his image from her mind.

6. A vivid or graphic description 1522.

7. (Rhetoric) A simile, metaphor, or figure of speech. 1676.

It will be enough to list the meanings of 'Imagery' detailed under heading 1. These are:

Images collectively; carved figures or decorations; image-work . . . (b) Figured work on a textile fabric, as in tapestry . . . (c) *trans*. The pictorial elements of a natural scene or landscape; scenery; nature's image-work. 1647 H. More *Poems*: As doth a looking-glasse (reflect) such imag'rie As it to the beholder doth detect. 1774 Warton: *History Of English Poetry*: Descriptive poetry and the representation of rural imagery.

What is lacking in these lists is a classification which will include the meaning 'Immediate object of sense-perception' (i.e. 'sense-datum'). The definition given under 'Image 3 b' is irrelevant because it is concerned with *deceptive* appearances: Dryden's Forms 'cheat' the sight. Definition number 5 is also beside the point, for the mental representations in question there are not the result of direct perception. And category 1 c under 'Imagery' does not meet our need, for we are not concerned exclusively with the *pictorial* element in sense-data; and in any case the definition here is not intended to apply to the

94

cognate 'image'. Hobbes's usage, already quoted, is simply not covered:

> 'Because the *Image* in Vision consisting of *Colour* and *Shape* is the knowledge we have of the qualities of the Object of that sense . . .'

When we consider the bearing this use of the word has on the history of English philosophy, it is odd indeed that the Dictionary should have taken no account of it. The omission may be partly explained by the insistence of the phenomenalists themselves that images inhere 'in the mind' and not in objects. But this is far from being an adequate explanation; for whether or not sense-images exist objectively in fact, they certainly seem to do so, whereas memory-images and pictures in the imagination (with occasional exceptions) do not. Hobbes acknowledges that the characteristics of sense-images are not simply the same as those of memory-images or images fabricated by imagination, though he applies the same *word* to all of them and claims that they are all subjective. Whenever he uses the word 'image' he specifies what *kind* of image he is referring to. And just as well; otherwise he would have confused his readers hopelessly.

Unlike Hobbes and the phenomenalists Wordsworth does justice to the manifest inherence of sense-images in things. He takes over the meaning 'immediate object of sense-perception' and deepens and complicates it; so that image (i.e. sense-image) comes to mean neither 'object of perception' simply nor 'object' simply, neither 'appearance' nor 'thing', but a fusion or amalgam (it is impossible to find an adequate metaphor—at any rate a single metaphor—in crabbed, discursive prose) of both.

This new meaning of 'image', which likewise goes unrecognized in the Dictionary, may be called a specifically

Romantic meaning: for an equivalent of it is to be found occasionally in the philosophical writings of Coleridge. (On the rare occasions when Coleridge uses the word 'image' in his poetry the meaning is familiar and simple: see *Reflections on having left a Place of Retirement* and *Lewti*. Coleridge the poet does not 'question' his sensations as Wordsworth does.) Since I began this essay by claiming that there is point in associating Wordsworth's poetry with Coleridge's philosophical speculations, it will be worth quoting some examples to illustrate how Coleridge could make the word 'image' yield much more than its normal (eighteenth-century) sense. In his *Treatise on Method* he writes:

'Events and images, the lively and spirit-stirring machinery of the external world, are like light, and air, and moisture, to the seed of the Mind, which would else rot and perish. In all processes of mental evolution the objects of the senses must stimulate the Mind; and the Mind must in turn assimilate and digest the food which it receives from without.'

These images are both the machinery of the external world and immaterial existences in the mind, and so may legitimately be compared to food, which is tangible before it is taken into the body but ceases to be so after digestion: Coleridge relies on both meanings of the word (realist and idealist) in order to persuade us that the mind actually draws into itself a part of its environment, as a plant does. True, 'image' often bears a conventional meaning in Coleridge's writing—as here, where the use of the word is Addisonian:

'On the other hand, in the poems which are pitched in a lower key, as the HARRY GILL, and THE IDIOT BOY, the feelings are those of human nature in general; though the poet has judiciously laid the scene in the country, in

96

order to place himself in the vicinity of interesting images, without the necessity of ascribing a sentimental perception of their beauty to the persons of his drama.'

(*Biographia Literaria*, Chap. XVII)

But when he uses the word in a philosophical context its connotation is apt to be less simple. There is an interesting transitional usage in a Notebook written at Malta (17.76, Coleridge notebooks in the British Museum) where the meaning of the word itself is conventional but the context indicates clearly how very ready Coleridge was to deepen and amplify that meaning:

'I work hard, I do the duties of common Life from morn to night/ but verily "I raise my limbs, like lifeless *Tools*." The organs of motion & outward action perform their functions at the stimulus of a galvanic fluid applied by the *Will*, not by the Spirit of Life that makes Soul and Body one. Thought and Reality two distinct corresponding Sounds, of which no man can say positively which is the Voice and which the Echo. O the beautiful Fountain or natural Well at Upper Stowey! The images of the weeds which hung down from its sides, appeared as plants growing up, straight and upright, among the water weeds that really grew from the Bottom/ & so vivid was the Image, that for some moments & not till after I had disturbed the water, did I perceive that their roots were not neighbours, & they side-by-side companions. So—even then I said—so are the happy man's *Thoughts* and *Things*—(in the language of the modern Philosophers, Ideas and Impressions.)—'

Or, as he had stated the matter in a letter to Sotheby (10 Sept, 1802):

'. . . a Poet's *Heart* & *Intellect* should be *combined, intimately* combined & *unified* with the great appearances of Nature, and not merely held in solution and loose mixture with them.'

Given these philosophical beliefs about the ideal relation of Thought and Thing, the meaning of 'image' in Coleridge's writing is bound now and then to strain beyond the limits imposed upon it by eighteenth-century philosophy. In the fragment *On Poesy or Art* we find him observing:

'In the objects of nature are presented, as in a mirror, all the possible elements, steps, and processes of intellect antecedent to consciousness, and therefore to the full development of the intelligential act; and man's mind is the very focus of all the rays of intellect which are scattered throughout the images of nature. Now so to place these images, totalized, and fitted to the limits of the human mind, as to elicit from, and to superinduce upon, the forms themselves the moral reflexions to which they approximate, to make the external internal, the internal external, to make nature thought, and thought nature,—this is the mystery of genius in the Fine Arts . . .'

These images of nature could no more inhabit a Cartesian universe than Wordsworth's could. Coleridge's strength as a philosopher, like Wordsworth's strength as a poet, was related intimately to his feeling for the equivocal nature of perception.

I hope to have shown in the foregoing pages that the study of the image has necessarily entailed an *evaluation* of Wordsworth's poetry. And indeed it would otherwise scarcely have been worth undertaking. Although I have been concerned to some extent with quasi-philosophical matters, and although my first object has been the simple one of indicating what the image is like and where it is to be found, I have inevitably been led on to the making of critical judgments on the poetry. To point to the dubiety of meaning in the word 'image' in the concluding passage of *The Ruined Cottage* for instance is to go some distance towards explaining why the poetry here is so powerful. Or consider the lines in *The Prelude* describing how the young Wordsworth suddenly felt himself to be 'A dedicated Spirit':

> Magnificent
> The morning was, in memorable pomp,
> More glorious than I ever had beheld.
> The Sea was laughing at a distance; all
> The solid Mountains were as bright as clouds,
> Grain-tinctured, drench'd in empyrean light;
> And, in the meadows and the lower grounds,
> Was all the sweetness of a common dawn,
> Dews, vapours, and the melody of birds,
> And Labourers going forth into the fields.

The sense of spiritual exaltation here is for the most part conveyed obliquely, and nothing witnesses more effectively to the perfect marriage of earth and heaven than the aspect of the mountains—solid, and yet so drenched in light as to seem like clouds. To draw attention to the ambiguity of the 'imagery' here is at the same time to indicate why the poetry is conspicuously successful.

It is on this note, appreciative more than expository, that I would like to end this essay; and I add two more examples from *The Prelude* to show how dubieties of meaning contribute to rich and noble effects.

99

Ye Presences of Nature, in the sky
And on the earth! Ye Visions of the hills!
And Souls of lonely places! can I think
A vulgar hope was yours when Ye employ'd
Such ministry, when Ye through many a year
Haunting me thus among my boyish sports,
On caves and trees, upon the woods and hills,
Impress'd upon all forms the characters
Of danger or desire, and thus did make
The surface of the universal earth
With triumph, and delight, and hope, and fear,
Work like a sea?

Could Wordsworth have contrived these supple transpositions
of feeling and sensation, and the exciting rhetoric which carries
us with such impetus to that strong and ecstatic half-line at the
conclusion, if he had not prepared the way with an un-
obtrusive transition from 'caves and trees . . . woods and hills'
to the ever-equivocal 'forms'? In the first book of *The Prelude*
such passages are particularly easy to find.

> Yet should these hopes
> Be vain, and thus should neither I be taught
> To understand myself, nor thou to know
> With better knowledge how the heart was fram'd
> Of him thou lovest, need I dread from thee
> Harsh judgments, if I am so loth to quit
> Those recollected hours that have the charm
> Of visionary things, and lovely forms
> And sweet sensations that throw back our life
> And almost make our Infancy itself
> A visible scene, on which the sun is shining?

There would appear to be nothing very remarkable about the

metaphor around which these lines are constructed (compare for instance *The Pleasures Of The Imagination* III, 300). And yet by the time we have reached them—they occur at the end of the book—'visionary', 'forms', 'sensations' and 'scene' have become so loaded with ambivalent meanings that Wordsworth can achieve here, with the simplest of verbal gestures, an effect of surprising complexity and power. His language in *The Prelude* and elsewhere embodies a more subtle play of mind than is usually conceded—even by his admirers.